Women
What the Hell are You Thinking Now?
Transform Your Thinking to Transform Your Life

CHERYL LACEY DONOVAN

Women, What the Hell are You Thinking Now?

CHERYL LACEY DONOVAN

Peace In The Storm Publishing, LLC

Giving Your Soul a Rise...One Page at a Time

Copyright © 2011 Cheryl Lacey Donovan

ISBN-13: 978-0-9829672-6-3

Library of Congress Control Number: 2011921628

PUBLISHER'S NOTE

Printed and bound in the United States of America. All rights reserved. No part of this book may be reproduced or transmitted in any form or by any means, electronic or mechanical, including photocopying, recording, or by an information storage and retrieval system-except by a reviewer who may quote brief passages in a review to be printed in a magazine, newspaper, or on the Web-without permission in writing from the publisher.

Although the author and publisher have made every effort to ensure the accuracy and completeness of information contained in this book, we assume no responsibility for errors, inaccuracies, omissions, or any inconsistency herein.

PEACE IN THE STORM PUBLISHING, LLC.
P.O. Box 1152
Pocono Summit, PA 18346

Visit our Web site at
www.PeaceInTheStormPublishing.com

Dedication

Scripture tells us God knows the plans He has for us but many times I hear people ask the question, "Why am I here? What is my purpose?" In other words He may know the plans but we don't.

Not knowing the answer to these questions causes many people to wander around in life aimlessly with no direction, no real focus. But there is a way to identify what you were placed on earth to do. Truthfully, many of us already know but we've allowed the enemy to fill us with the spirit of fear and thwart the manifestation of God's vision in us here on earth. But you can re-kindle the vision. You can rediscover God's will for your life. How by following a few biblical guidelines that can help point you in the direction of God's plans for you.

Women What the Hell are You Thinking Now is dedicated to those women who find themselves not knowing. Use this book and the resources that accompany it to discover your divine purpose. Reclaim your dream. Reclaim your destiny. Reclaim your life. It is the will of God for you.

Acknowledgements

First and foremost I acknowledge my savior and redeemer for without Him I would be nothing. It is He who gives me strength to endure, power to persevere, and wisdom to share.

To my family and friends thank you for your continued undying support.

To the Peace in the Storm family we've come to far to turn back now.

May God continue to richly bless you all.

PRAISE FOR
Women, What the Hell are You Thinking Now?

Cheryl, you speak with authority, wisdom, and experience. Your book is certain to breathe life into those who feel beaten down by circumstances. Your strong yet loving words will draw women of all ages and stages to the power and peace that only our Risen Lord can provide. He has spoken through you. Thank you for being an obedient messenger. In Christ's love and warmth,
~Jory H. Fisher, JD, www.WomenFindPurpose.com

Cheryl Lacey Donovan has a powerful voice with her ministry of words. Donovan has crafted *Women, What the Hell are You Thinking Now?* with the academic spirit of a theologian, yet she gracefully manifests the information with a gentleness only a virtuous woman can render. Much more than a quick read, *Women, What the Hell are You Thinking Now?* is an experience and the beginnings of a powerful lifestyle for any woman open to learn the fullness of her Christian potential in the eyes of God. With this book, Donovan gives you the tools to recycle the harsh inadequacies of your past into a glorious future for the Kingdom, your family, your friends...and YOU.
~Joey Pinkney, Author and Book Reviewer

INTRODUCTION

Webster's defines 'virtuous' as conformity to a standard of right. Most of us have heard of the "Virtuous Woman" found in Proverbs Chapter 31. She's the pinnacle of Christian womanhood. She's upright, strong, courageous, wise, and kind. She's every woman's model of what a woman should be. She's faithful and industrious and she fears God. She's strong and able to endure. She knows when it's time to watch, when it's time to fight, and when it's time to pray. Her self-esteem is high because she knows that she's a child of the King and that she's more than a conqueror through Jesus Christ. She believes no weapon formed against her will prosper and God can make her enemies her footstool even in the most trying of circumstances. A virtuous woman would never allow a man to rob her of her dignity or her virtue by sleeping around, acquiescing to domestic violence, or sleeping with him when he's married. A virtuous woman would know these things are not of God because they demean her self-worth and tear down her communication with the Almighty. A virtuous woman would also be wise enough to know that after everything she's done, her God is a forgiving God and He's faithful to His Word.

Women are more than sugar and spice and everything nice. They are fearfully and wonderfully made by God and we women need to learn how to align our view of ourselves with God's view of us. Far too often we allow the situations in our lives to consume us and tear us down. But, this isn't the will of God for our lives. God's plans for us are always good and we need to review those plans and incorporate them into our daily living. If you're not satisfied with where you are in life, then it's time to for you to develop a new way of thinking that lines up with God's will.

Now that we know who we are and whose we are let's be real. Women, what in the hell are you thinking; and I do mean hell, because the situations we allow ourselves to be placed in are straight from the pit of hell designed by the enemy himself to take us out. They're planned by the powers and principalities of Satan to undermine the order of God and the woman's divine position in that order.

The Bible is full of strong, righteous, courageous, God fearing, women: Esther, who put her life on the line for her people, Deborah who was a fearless leader, and Hannah who prayed for what she wanted and received favor from God. These were women who were faced with issues of life; twists and turns that could've surely taken them off course and yet they found a way to seek God's face and persevere.

Being the backbones of their families we see even in Proverbs 31:13- 27, the Bible speaks of the important roles women play in the lives of their families. They're the caretakers of their homes speaking with wisdom, they set about their work vigorously and their arms are strong for their tasks; yet, many of us suffer with low self-esteem, broken hearts, wounded souls and dead spirits. We don't live in the glory of our divine placement. We personify an outward appearance of happiness, while living in pure hell on the inside. To the naked eye we seem joyful, courageous and in control while on the inside we're scared little girls wishing somebody, anybody, would rescue us. We need to take our lives back. God wants to restore us. He wants to reconstruct what's been broken down. What looks like trash in your life can be recycled and bring about reformation and restoration. You've gone through the devastation of divorce, disease, loss of friends, family and finances. You're looking at what's left after using external solutions to fix internal chaos and you think it's all over. Instead of getting to the root of the problem you just prune the outside branches. Leading to our detriment too often we engage in continuous patterns of over eating, indulging in chemical fixes – alcohol, drugs, smoking, over working, using our career to identify who we are, rescuing people, being a savior, expecting too little, putting up walls, emotional distancing, people pleasing. Ultimately, we suffer from controlling behavior, distrust, perfectionism, intimacy problems. Or even worse, we form ungodly attachments to people or mindsets of un- forgiveness, bitterness, and malice.

Women what in hell are you thinking now? As long as you allow these things to control your life, you'll be stuck in a never-ending pit that will engulf you and never release you unless you come to realize you are daughters of the King, daughters of the Most High God. It's time to get rid of the clutter. Don't be consumed by fear. It's not of God. Man doesn't have a heaven or hell to send you to, so walking in a place of people pleasing can only hinder you from receiving what God has for you. As long as you keep allowing the same difficulties to consume you your life will be crowded, confused, disordered and full of junk. Don't be conformed to this world but transform yourself by the renewing of your mind. Get rid of negative self- talk and negative self-images that keep playing themselves over and over in your head. Align yourself with God's Word and see the amazing transformation that can take place in your life. No, this doesn't mean that every day will be rosy, but your outlook and your perspective, even in the center of tumultuous times, will be joyous because you know that God is still in control in the midst of it all. As long as you trust in Him all things will work together for good.

Trying to push you down, life will cause you to face disappointments and setbacks. Reminiscing on past failure will cloud your mind deceiving you into falsely believing you haven't been or can't be forgiven for past transgressions. Trusting God seems impossible because you still believe He's forgotten about you in the quagmire of your troubles. The issues of life; bad news concerning your health, a relationship that went south, -unemployment – all of these are setbacks. Discouragement, loss of enthusiasm, temptation to settle where you are all things that keep drawing your focus away from the things of God and places it squarely on the things that weigh you down. But if you're going to see the best out of life, you have to have a "bounce-back" mentality. Knocked down, you don't stay down. You get back up again. You don't get bitter, you get better. You have to know that every time hardship comes, your setback is a setup for a comeback!

Your spirit may be trying to get you to commit suicide. But in these pages, I speak life to your spirit and remind you that God has deposited too much in you for you to die. It's time for you to make a withdrawal. Psalm 118:17 says, "I shall not die, but live, and declare the works of the Lord." Do the work God has ordained for you to do. Be about your Father's business!

Pity parties, depression, soaking yourself in the cares of this world, blaming everyone else for your problems, none of this will get you any closer to the life God has planned for you. The kingdom is waiting for you to position yourself for the greatness God has in store. Days and days of sitting and pondering on what you're going through are over. Cast your cares upon God, knowing that he cares for you. I Peter 5:7. Everything happens, everything exists, and everything was created to give God glory. Even your struggles are an opportunity for God to get the glory.

Weeping endures for a night but JOY comes in the morning. There's a plan and destiny that God has for you. Chief Architect of your life, He's building you up to be all He's purposed you to be.

God is revealing the glory through your suffering, through your pain, through your bondage situation. He's

Women, What the Hell are You Thinking Now?

establishing you in the midst of what you're going through. Push through to your destiny!

You are pregnant with purpose, pregnant with greatness. Allow the baby to be born. Don't permit the enemy to abort your vision. God has deposited something great on the inside of you and it's time for your delivery! Let the weak say I'm strong and the poor say I'm rich; Rich with the power of the Spirit, Rich with the Word of God, Rich with health, Rich with strength and courage. Take authority over the enemy and declare dominion over everything God has for you. Reclaim your purpose, reclaim your hopes, reclaim your destiny, and reclaim your dreams!

God has a big life for you, one that has peace, joy, and wholeness. His plan includes love and value, purpose and fulfillment, provision and supply. Whatever has caused you to be broken, the areas in your life that aren't working or are ineffective, the areas where you feel powerless, doing nothing and going nowhere, God wants to put them back together again! But you can't get to the upper level when you're stuck on the ground floor.

The pages that follow will speak to the inner recesses of your soul and cause you to really look at yourself in a way that perhaps you've never done before. This introspection will force you to stand up and take notice of the woman that God has called you to be and to never again allow Satan to trick you into the behaviors of the past. Even if you aren't where you want to be right now, don't despair. God isn't through with you yet. You are a unique woman with a unique plan designed by God just for you. *Women What the Hell are You Thinking Now* uses life lessons and biblical principles that will inspire you to walk in the life God has ordained for you. I pray that this book will help you to become whole in your mind, your body, and your spirit.

WHAT ARE YOU THINKING?

So as a man thinketh in his heart so is he. Proverbs 23:7.

The enemy loves to put thoughts into our minds and if we're not careful, those thoughts produce strongholds so your decisions will ultimately reflect in your actions by moving you in the wrong direction. Your soul is the primary point at which the enemy deposits words that are in direct opposition to what God says. It's within your soul that your mind, will and emotions reside. The enemy's goal is to infect your mind. Lies are the weapons of mass destruction the devil uses to threaten and intimidate you. They're the prison bars he uses to lock you up in sin, sickness, sorrow and lack—all the things from which Jesus has set you free! When sickness attacks us, the devil lies to us and says, "This sickness is just your cross to bear. God wants to use it to teach you something." When we encounter financial needs, the devil lies and says, "You're never going to find a better job, poverty is just God's way of keeping you humble." When we're in trouble and need deliverance, the devil lies to us and says, "God won't help you out of this situation because it's your own fault. God wants to teach you a lesson." The devil will keep telling you these lies over and over again until they become part of your reality. But the truth of God's Word proves it's all a deception. It tells us plainly that Jesus came that we might have life and have it more abundantly.

Without interruption, our minds are consistently infiltrated with two voices that are speaking. Satan tempts us daily by applying pressure to our thinking patterns that if allowed to continue will explode in a mess too large to contain. He skillfully and manipulatively plants seeds of suggestion that root themselves and grow into manifested temptation either through things we enjoy or through things we've walked away from.

Years after I went through my pregnancy as a teen and experienced the abuse of domestic violence, I would replay the negative messages of the past repetitively in my mind. In the process, I questioned my own sense of judgment and my ability to overcome. "How could I be so stupid? How could I stay as long as I did? How could I not see who he really was? I could be so much further along if I had just listened."

Satan wanted me to be reminded of how woefully inadequate I really was. He said, "You're broken and defeated you're a failure, you're a disappointment." But Jesus, through God's Word, told me that if I turned to Him, I'd be forgiven and my past forgotten: Isaiah 43:25, "I, even I, am he that blotteth out thy transgressions for mine own sake, and will not remember thy sins."

I was faced with a choice: I could either listen to Satan's lie that I was a failure and a disappointment, or I could listen to God's Word telling me my past was washed away and I was a new creature in Christ! 2 Corinthians 5:17, "Therefore if any man be in Christ, he is a new creature: old things are passed away; behold, all things are become new."

I chose to listen to God's voice and allowed it to crowd out the voice of the enemy. I chose to walk in the knowledge that my battle wasn't carnal, It wasn't against the people and the circumstances in my life, It was the enemy operating through those people and circumstances to get me isolated and drawn away from my destiny. Listening to the enemy had only brought me heartache. It left me disillusioned, confused, and troubled. Nothing in my life to this point was headed in the right direction because I had chosen not to listen to the precepts and examples that had been set before me in the Word. I was on a road, a crossroad. If I didn't choose the right path this time I would end up in oblivion. Thinking good thoughts wasn't enough to turn my life around. I had to ward off Satan's temptation and stop it from progressing by casting down its attempts with God's Word. In other words, it's easy to say, "Satan, I rebuke you," but you need a little more than that to ward off his attacks. You need to be able to speak a Word from God specific to your situation because He's already promised His Word will not return to Him void. Ministering angels are waiting to hear those words and assist you in your battle against the evil one, but you have to take the authority given you and use it.

The strongholds in our lives are built on the foundation created by the lies of the enemy. But when we feast on the truth in God's Word, it tears down the strongholds and makes it harder for the enemy's voice to penetrate the walls of our thoughts. Opposing thoughts should never be allowed to take root in our minds. If we allow them to grow like weeds in a garden of roses, they will eventually choke the life out of us.

Listening to Satan's decrees that I was a failure would've continued to feed that lie, until it grew into strongholds of poverty, reliance on government assistance,

Women, What the Hell are You Thinking Now?

low self-esteem, and decreased confidence in my ability to move forward in my purpose. My feelings would've been a direct result of my thoughts, ultimately concluding in a self-fulfilling prophecy. But listening to my Father in heaven , who was speaking truth to me through His Word, I began to tear down the strongholds in my life and rebuild a future based on wisdom, knowledge and understanding. Those messages from society that kept playing ever so relentlessly in my head telling me I would be on welfare, living in government housing with children who wouldn't graduate high school or worse; who would be in prison the rest of their lives, crumbled under the weight of the Word of God . When I meditated on the truth in God's Word, it became part of me, and before long, I began feeling different, simply because I was exchanging lies of the devil for the truth in God's Word. I believed my sins were forgiven and I allowed my conscience to be cleansed from dead works by the blood of Jesus: Hebrews 9:14, "How much more shall the blood of Christ, who through the eternal Spirit offered himself without spot to God, purge your conscience from dead works to serve the living God?"

    I refused to end up feeling like a loser... guilt-ridden by my past. I turned a deaf ear to the simple voice of condemnation from the enemy. Satan's network of evil spirits wants to interject thoughts into your mind that remind you of your mistakes, missteps, misfortune and missed opportunities. Don't listen to his voice and agree with it. You may have sinned, even failed. But I challenge you to look at the solution which is repentance and the blood of Jesus. Don't continue to listen to the enemy who keeps reminding you of your shortcomings, because once a stronghold or incorrect thinking pattern based on lies and formed in deception has captured your thoughts, you'll start believing the deception instead of believing the truth of God's Word, which tells you that you've been forgiven and washed clean, and that even God, Himself, has chosen to forget your dirty past!

You're a child of God who's washed clean in the blood of Jesus. You're not unworthy, guilty or a loser. Believe it because whatever you keep your mind on will affect your whole being. Isaiah 26:3, "Thou wilt keep him in perfect peace, whose mind is stayed on thee: because he trusteth in thee."

Women what are you thinking? Because whatever you're thinking will become magnified in your eyes and in your life. Whatever you give heed to, will become more important to you than anything else. Guard your mind because it doesn't take much to open your eyes and see why so many Christians are living defeated lives and walk around guilt-ridden, lacking the joy of the Lord in their lives.

Without that joy, where is their strength supposed to come from? After all, as Nehemiah 8:10 tells us, "For the joy of the Lord is your strength."

That's why the enemy tries to get your mind and thoughts derailed off the truth. He tries to get you to worry about things that in reality, you have no reason to be worried about! Are you having a problem with sin? That's been dealt with in 1 John 1:9, "If we confess our sins, he is faithful and just to forgive us our sins, and to cleanse us from all unrighteousness." In plain English, it doesn't matter what you've done, if you're willing to take it before the Lord, you can be forgiven! Is your money looking funny? God supplies all your needs according to His riches in glory and He is the one who gives you the ability to get wealth. Deuteronomy 8:18, "But thou shalt remember the LORD thy God: for it is he that giveth thee power to get wealth, that he may establish his covenant which he swore unto thy fathers, as it is this day." Are you sick in your body? Then by His stripes you are healed. God has given His promises for every area of your life. It's up to you to know those promises and stand on them when the enemy comes to capture your mind.

The biggest difference between a victorious believer and a defeated believer is the very thoughts that go through their mind. Demon spirits can, and do, play a big role in depression and fear. Many times all they have to do is get our thoughts off track. When that happens, because of our ignorance of the truth, we begin to become fearful and depressed. Fear and depression are often at the primary basis of the spiritual warfare tactic used by evil spirits. Saul was tormented by evil spirits who caused fear and depression to sweep over him. 1 Samuel 16:14, "Now the Spirit of the LORD had left Saul, and the LORD sent a tormenting spirit that filled him with depression and fear.

Is depression part of God's plan for you? No! He wants you to be joyful! Should fear dictate our path? No! He wants us to rest in His love, which expels all fear! We have not been given a spirit of fear again to bondage, but of power and love and a sound mind! His Word in 2 Timothy 1:7 is evidence of that. Can worry and anxiety bring about a change on our lives? No! His Word tells us not to worry about anything! Philippians 4:6-8 paints the picture quite well between thoughts and feelings, "Be careful for nothing; but in everything by prayer and supplication with thanksgiving let your requests be made known unto God. And the peace of God, which passeth all understanding, shall keep your hearts and minds through Christ Jesus."

I am a witness that refusing to worry about anything opens the door to God's peace in our lives. People often say to me, "Why are you always smiling? Why does it seem like nothing ever goes wrong in your life?" It's because I choose to set my mind on good and positive things that uplift me and build me up. Isaiah 26:3 makes a vital connection between what we fix our minds on, and how we feel, "Thou wilt keep him in perfect peace, whose mind is stayed on thee: because he trusteth in thee." Do you think God is in heaven worried about anything? If He isn't worried about it, why should we worry about it? Hasn't he said we are His children; joint heirs with Christ?

Here's what we should be thinking about: Colossians 3:2, "Set your affection on things above, not on things on the earth." To set your affection on something in the Greek means to exercise the mind. Instead of concentrating on negative things and worrying about things we can't change, let's begin to do as God's Word says and meditate in our minds on positive things that encourage, inspire, and enrich us. Instead of looking at the problems in our lives; sin, poverty, and sickness; let's begin looking at the solutions; forgiveness, blessings, and healing. We can find all this and more in Jesus!

Take inventory of the thoughts that have recently entered your mind. What kind of thoughts were they; negative- problem focused, dealing with the cares of this world? Have they mostly been thoughts that tear you down and keep your eyes on the problem? Or were they positive thoughts that have built you up? How much time have you been spending thinking about the goodness of God and how God is your healer, deliverer, and provider?

Stop looking at the problems in your life, and begin looking at the solutions that God has provided for you as His child! Get your mind off the problem and on to the solution! If it's a healing you need, then begin to research the scriptures to learn what God's Word has to say about healing. If it's finances you need, then begin to research the Word and see what it has to say about your finances and God's provision for you. Seek God's Word on the matter. For Jesus said that whosoever shall you seek, you shall find Matthew 7:7. Notice that Jesus didn't say "Sit there and think about the problem and the solution will come on its own."

As I began to claim my mind back from the enemy, he didn't want to give it up. I had to battle against the confusion he wrought with the weapons of my warfare; prayer, praise, and scripture. I began to declare out loud that no one, and nothing, would think for me. I started thinking about what I was thinking about so I could discern the lies of the enemy that had been planted there to take me off course. As I identified his lies, I confessed the truth out loud. As my spirit became healthier, I experienced more peace and more joy. My nights became more restful, and the ability to concentrate and comprehend became more attainable.

Women, What the Hell are You Thinking Now?

You're in a battle, yet you're not alone. The enemy doesn't want to relinquish his hold on your mind so it will be difficult to win. But you have to remember to call on God's grace in the Name of Jesus, and He will give you the power of the Holy Spirit to overcome. Regaining your mind is a process, but don't give up. Continue claiming what belongs to you; your mind and your thinking.

Women what are you thinking?

WHAT'S IN YOUR HOUSE?

What know ye not that your body is the temple of the Holy Ghost which is in you, which ye have of God and ye are not your own? For ye are bought with a price, therefore, glorify God in your body, and in your spirit, which are God's. 1 Corinthians 6:19-20.

Ungodly alliances, ungodly attachments, ungodly mindsets, ungodly thoughts; what lives in your house? Life's most complicated issues are often a direct reflection of what we allow to live in our temple; our house. Friends and relations who mean us no good, negative self-talk, and attitudes that stop us before we even get started, all clutter our existence with mindsets of unclean thoughts, convoluted ideas, and clouded vision.

CHERYL LACEY DONOVAN

Believers understand, and perhaps accept, they are forgiven; yet we are not whole. We don't walk in the anointing or live the abundant lives Jesus died for because we're fragmented spiritually, emotionally, and mentally. Our identity is distorted because we have no clue as to who we really are. We don't look at ourselves as daughters of the King, children of the Most High God. Defenseless, because we don't have the faith to believe everything works out for our good. We run like scared little children into the darkness that encompasses our souls. Not knowing why we're here pushes us into feelings of not being accepted and disillusionment about our purpose. We wander around in a fog, trying to fit in, only to find we've traveled further away from our true destination.

The walls of our temple, our house, have been pummeled by the issues of life. The foundation is cracked and faulty because boundaries have been crossed and we've allowed the enemy into our camp through bad relationships, poor choices, and misguided steps. We've given him permission to invade our territory and mess up our house. The trash has piled up producing a heap of unwanted debris crowding out all the valuables we've stored on the inside. Threatening our ability to be more Christ like, more like the women God intended doubt, fear, lust, resentment and jealousy, shaped by traumatic experiences of divorce, death,

Women, What the Hell are You Thinking Now?

years of abuse, bankruptcy, rape and other tragedies of life, have left us with pain we can't describe; a purpose in peril. Hoarding disappointment, bitterness, anger and self-defeat we find ourselves unable to dig our way out. Longing for God's presence, we seek His promises only to be left on the side of the road feeling passed by.

Your position has been compromised and your power is lost. But I stopped here to tell you all things; even the bad, work together for the good of those who love God and are called according to His purposes. It's time to clean out the clutter; time to get rid of the confusion, the disorder, the chaos. It's time to rebuild the wall and kick the enemy out of your house as you build a clear line of defense against the adversary and your flesh.

I never thought anything good could come out of being physically abused by a man. I never thought anything good could come out of being pregnant at the age of sixteen. I asked the same question the people asked about Jesus when they said, "Can anything good come out of Nazareth?" "God, I said, can anything good come out of my pain?" Can anything good come out of my disappointment?" The answer is a resounding, yes!

The enemy's desire, the enemy's plan, yes he has plans for us too, was to keep me from experiencing all God had for me. He wanted to keep me wallowing in the pit of my despair, with no hope and no reason to expect breakthrough. He wanted me to give in to the agony and the hurt I was feeling, so he could get my eyes off Jesus, and onto me and my issues. He wanted me to look away from what God was doing long enough that I would never experience the fullness of joy that God intended for me. He wanted my mind to be filled with my problems, instead of God's promises. Nevertheless, I realized everything I'd been through didn't destroy me! I was still here and God was calling me to something greater. The enemy couldn't keep destiny down in my life as long as I didn't allow him to control my thoughts and emotions. I stopped cursing my crisis because it was part of my ultimate destiny.

Clear the clutter from your house and discern God's true will for your life. There's purpose in the pain. Stop taking matters in your own hands just because you can only see as far as your present. Remember, God can see into your future. God's purpose will prevail if you let it. Don't be your own worst enemy. Don't stand in your own way.

Aligning ourselves with God helps us fulfill our need for meaning; our need for purpose. Stop playing with the poison in your life and instead breakthrough with force from the bondage that's held you captive. Whatever restricted you in the past is being removed as you change your way of thinking and walk in the destiny God has prepared for you. Clear your house of spiritual clutter, issues, mindsets, past history, and habits that have held you shackled to the chains of hopelessness. Separate yourself from ungodly attachments and soul ties hindering you from escape. Stop allowing guilt and shame to keep you in relationships and situations that are chipping away your house walls and adding to the debris. Stop being a rescuer unless you're rescuing yourself, because you're only healing the symptoms when what you really need is to get to the root of the disease. Continuously providing us with lessons, life has a way of turning those lessons into problems. Problems become crisis, and crisis becomes chaos. Our only out is learning the lesson and purposely creating the life we desire. The power belongs to us and was given to us by the Almighty God. But too often we wait on Him to fix problems we can fix ourselves by making better choices and decisions.

God has given us the power to get wealth. He has given us everything we need to prosper. His desire is not that we perish, but that we live life more abundantly. Believe in what God has for you. Lay aside every weight and hindrance to your future. Trust in the Lord with all your heart. He will direct your path. Clean house!

IN THE EYE OF THE BEHOLDER

Who can find a virtuous woman for her price is far above rubies. Proverbs 31:10.

In this particular proverb, Solomon asks a poignant question. As you consider this, I'd like each of you to picture in your mind a virtuous woman. Just take about 60 seconds to do so. Now, how many of you pictured yourself?

Why is it that when we talk about a virtuous woman we think of Big Mama, Mama, Aunt Ruby, the lady down the street; any and every woman except ourselves?

Walking down the hall, watching television, and flipping through magazines; how do you decide who's beautiful? Is it long hair; a size 6 figure that won't quit? We buy into this fantasy of beauty, spending all our money on lipo, weave, and a new pair of eyes. This image of the ideal woman is so deeply embedded in our society that cosmetic surgeons are becoming millionaires in droves as a result. Why is it we feel this woman is so attainable, yet, the woman that Solomon speaks of is so unreachable? Now, don't misunderstand me ladies, it's perfectly okay to want to look good and feel good about yourself, but don't be fooled, the bible tells us that grace is deceitful and beauty is vain. The true beauty of a woman of God is that she loves and fears the Lord. One writer has written, a woman isn't born a woman, nor does she become one when she marries a man, bears a child and does their dirty laundry; not even when she joins a women's liberation movement. A woman becomes a woman when she becomes what God wants her to be.

Commercials, newspapers, magazines, and reality TV have fooled us into believing that all of these material things are a true measure of our worth. We've skewed our thinking as to what true beauty is. And until we begin to see ourselves the way God sees us, we're destined to be held in bondage to cosmetic surgeons, foreign hair companies, exercise gurus and others who profit from our poor self-image; an image fueled by our lack of understanding of who we are and how we were made.

1 Samuel 16:7 finds Saul, rejected by God as King of Israel, because of his disobedience. God then sends Samuel to Jesse's home to anoint a new king. As Samuel gets to Jesse's house, he immediately sees Jesse's oldest son, whose name was Eliab. Without hesitation, Samuel thinks, "This must be the next king of Israel! He's tall, handsome and striking. He has the swagger of a King. He's stately and regal in his manner." But God tells Samuel he mustn't look at the outside to determine who's to be the next king. It's the inside that counts to God!

Believing appearance to be everything, we conclude if it looks good then it must be good. Realistically, however, everything that looks good to you isn't good for you. God reminds us time and time again throughout scripture; it's the inside that counts.

So then how does the Bible view beauty? Let's start with Solomon's definition. What does this passage tell us about beauty? Solomon says that a virtuous woman's price is far above rubies. Now why do you think Solomon would define a woman's worth in this way? Well, in my quest to answer this question, I learned several things about the word 'virtuous.' First of all the expression 'virtuous woman' is from the Hebrew Ishhah Chayil and literally means "one of power either in mind, body, or both." The dictionary points out that the word 'virtuous' is synonymous with the words, 'good' and 'worthy.' As we further study biblical characters such as Rachel, Deborah, and Hannah, we find that virtuous women exhibit certain characteristics that lead to victorious living. The virtuous woman is strong, courageous, wise and kind. She is faithful, industrious, and most of all she loves God. These women are caretakers of their homes, they speak with wisdom, they set about their work vigorously, and their arms are strong for their tasks. These women don't sleep with other women's husband's, succumb to domestic violence, or settle for living on welfare, because they know that these things are not of God; and their wisdom teaches them that participating in these behaviors will only lead to a break down in their relationship with God. Therefore, Solomon is telling us that a good woman, a worthy woman, is hard to find. So that once you know that you have found her, she is priceless and should be treasured.

But the question still remains. Why rubies? What was so special about rubies? Now, I know that rubies can be expensive and in some cases even priceless. So, when Solomon, being the wise man that he was, says that 'our worth' is far above rubies, I think that he knew exactly what he was talking about because God sees us in the same way. Why else would He entrust us with His most precious

Women, What the Hell are You Thinking Now?

creation; mankind. God chose 'us,' women, to bring forth life. So, I know that He believes that we are priceless. So then why is it that so many of us live our lives as though we are worthless? In considering this fact, I went back to the verse and established that part of the problem, is that we are not living a virtuous life. And the reason for this is because we do not consider ourselves to be good or worthy. How do I know? Because if we felt like we were good enough, then we wouldn't allow ourselves to be lowered into thinking that sleepin' with a married man was okay. We wouldn't allow ourselves to live in abusive relationships. If we felt like the worthy women we are, we wouldn't be in the club walkin' it out, with a skirt up to our butt, and a blouse down to our navel leavin' with Jody who we know doesn't mean us any good. Naw, my sistas! That doesn't sound like someone that understands her worth.

Now, I went back to this passage and I asked myself, "Self?" and self said, "Yes." I went on questioning myself. "Just how much is a ruby worth?"

Well, being the internet geek that my husband says that I am, I found out from *a popular website on gemology* that many individuals consider the ruby to be especially precious among stones because of their rarity, their brilliant fire, and their rich color. With these types of qualities, you know that regardless of the ruby you choose, you will definitely receive a piece of jewelry that you will surely cherish for a lifetime. Rarity, brilliant fire, and rich color.

The color red, itself, has symbolized many different things to various cultures. Some of the interpretations of the color red include courage, passion, power, fire, and royalty. With these types of associations, how can you not love both the color and the brilliance of a fine and rare ruby?

And such it is with a good woman: a worthy woman, a woman who has courage, passion, power and fire. She's hard to find. So when you do find her, how can you not love and admire her brilliance and her rarity?

Now I couldn't just stop there as I examined the ruby. I needed to know exactly what a ruby was.

Now if all of this is true about rubies, then I needed to know how much then does a ruby cost. Well, depending on the color, cut, and clarity of individual rubies, the cost of a one-carat, ruby jewel can range in price from the very inexpensive, to thousands of dollars. In fact, some outstanding rubies are even more expensive than diamonds of a similar size when it comes to value. Well, guess what? The Bible says that the cost of a good woman is far greater than that, because she was bought, and paid for, with the blood of the Lamb. Aren't you glad, that unlike rubies, your color, your cut, and your clarity don't matter? Jesus paid the penalty for your sins on the cross a long time ago. He shed

Women, What the Hell are You Thinking Now?

His precious blood to redeem your soul from damnation. He rose, victorious form the grave, and He lives on high at the right hand of God, the Father. His strength is sufficient for you; both now and forever.

    Since the ruby is so costly, I found myself wondering exactly how a ruby was made. Surely, the creation of a ruby involved a great deal of work. So I went back to *the gems website t*o see if I could find out how a ruby was formed. What I found out was this: Rubies, themselves, are the red variety of a material known as corundum. In other colors it would be known as a sapphire. The popular red color of rubies is, in actuality, derived from small amounts of chromic oxide in the corundum, and when you are looking for one of the more valuable and rare rubies in existence, you will want to find one that is purely saturated with no hints of other colors such as brown or purple. In general, the most prized rubies are those rubies with an intense red color, and a great deal of brilliance.

    So you see when you find a good woman, this woman will be purely saturated in the Word of God, with no hints of outside influences. She will be sure of who she is, and whose she is. Her view of herself will be directly in line with God's view of her. Her God influenced confidence will be such that she can speak to the situations in her life and they will move out of her way. Even when her circumstances look grim, she will be like Paul, and say that she has learned to be content in all situations, knowing that God can and will bring her through.

Now, I don't want you to be deceived about rubies. Rubies that are perfect in appearance and color are extremely rare. Therefore, enhancements to rubies are quite commonplace. In other words, everybody can't be Mother Theresa. How then, you may ask are rubies enhanced? Well, heating is perhaps, one of the most popular ways of treating these precious gems. Through the heating process, the ruby improves with respect to the clarity of the jewel and/or the intensity of the red color. Since this type of treatment is quite stable, you, as a consumer, don't have to worry about the color of your treated ruby fading over time. How does that relate to women? Well, I'm glad you asked. It simply means that the ruby has to go through the fire, before it can emerge with some clarity and some intensity. That 'fire' may be in the form of bad marriages, unhealthy relationships, teenage pregnancy, drug abuse, or domestic violence. But when the fire is over; you will emerge with some clarity and some intensity.

Now, in my research, I discovered that there are times when some rubies have small cracks in them, and, as a result, they are filled with other materials. Unlike the heating enhancement, this type of enhancement can, for example, break or even fall out of the ruby entirely. This breakage is more likely to occur if the jewel is treated in a rough manner, exposed to high temperatures, or otherwise submersed in abrasive situations. Many of us find ourselves in abrasive situations just like the ruby because we've allowed men to hold way too much power over us because of the way they talk about us and our bodies, or even the way they look at us. Contrary to popular belief: ladies, we're not just pieces of meat and we shouldn't allow ourselves to be treated as such. You should want a man that will build you up and value you for who God has created you to be; in the manner that He considers to be amazingly stunning and beautiful. We should leave our physical looks out of it.

Many of us are just like Leah, lookin' for love in all the wrong places. Leah spent many years, longing to be loved by Jacob. In her mind, her very being came from Jacob's love. It took her years to figure out that the path she was on was a dead end. Many of us are so concerned about being loved by a man, that we give him permission to evaluate our self-worth. We allow him to treat us as he pleases with no consequences or repercussions. We settle for the fact that a piece of man is better than no man at all. We demean the very existence of God within us by being subjected to abuse of our bodies, our minds, and our very being. But listen, God is a faithful God, and he will forgive you of all of your sins if you just ask him. You may have some small cracks, but if you look to God, who is the author and finisher of your faith, you will emerge out of your abrasive situation and He will fill the cracks in your heart, your soul and your mind, so that you can emerge with fire, power, and brilliance. But remember, you have to let go of the feelings of anger, rage, bitterness and un-forgiveness. You have to let the Holy Spirit, help you to live according to God's perfect plan. You have to deal with the issues of your past so that they don't control your future. The only person that these negative feelings will hurt is you. Forgiving others and releasing anger, reconnects you with God and makes it possible for Him to guide you.

Now, I've got another question for you here. Based on how God views beauty and our bodies, should it change our perception about modifying our appearances, or the way we dress? This ranges from things as simple as dying our hair, getting piercings, tattoos, and weight lifting, but it also carries through to plastic surgery and steroids. Consider 1 Timothy 2:9-10, "In like manner also, that women adorn themselves in modest apparel, with shamefacedness and sobriety; not with braided hair, or gold, or pearls, or costly array; but which becometh women professing godliness with good works."

Women, What the Hell are You Thinking Now?

The context of both of these passages is a church setting, so the question here should be: What are your motives for going to church? The correct answer is to worship God! You shouldn't be like the women in these passages who had ulterior motives; motives involving drawing all the attention onto them; making themselves in reality; idols. The bottom line is this comes down to motives.

When it comes to clothes, the question is; why are you wearing what you're wearing? Are you wearing certain clothes because you like them or look good in them? Or are you wearing something to solely draw attention to yourself. Do you want to feel attractive, pretty and sexy? Why do you work out as much as you do? Are you working out to stay fit, healthy and toned? Or do you wear what you do because you want men lusting over you? As women, we should check our motives in all that we do.

Why do you dye your hair? Why do you get a piercing a tattoo? Etc. If your sole motivation on any of these is to just draw attention to yourself and try to get people to like you or notice you, then you're making your appearance an idol and trying to find your worth in it. To be honest, you won't ever find it.

This is a 'body conscious' world, but the Christian has another dimension to this attitude. The day you became a Christian, something happened to your body. Your body became the Temple of the Holy Spirit and should remind you of the temple in the Old Testament. Great care was given to its design. Immense wealth was placed into its construction. God dwelt there. But there's no such place in our day and time. The building is no longer God's Temple. The brick and mortar church is not where God dwells; it's just the place the people of God meet. Your body is God's Temple in this age of grace; be careful where it goes. Be careful what it does. Be careful what it ponders. Be careful how it reacts.

The Holy Spirit lives within His temple. You are His temple and His Spirit resides within you. The Holy Spirit is with you wherever you go. His power is available when you need it. Every word and deed is in His view. He is grieved at our inconsistencies. Let me give you an example; Have you ever had someone visit your home and put their dirty feet all over your furniture or go in your kitchen and open your refrigerator like they live there? Or maybe they put wet glasses on your newly polished coffee table and then looked at you daring you to respond. The tragedy here is that this is how we treat God's temple; our bodies. You're not your own. You were bought, with a price. God is the landlord of our body and soul and we treat Him as if He has no right to be there. The title to our house belongs to Him, and because of His grace and mercy, we're allowed to lease it on a day-

Women, What the Hell are You Thinking Now?

by-day basis. We have no rights or privileges, and we can be evicted at any time. We were fearfully and wonderfully made by God. And God don't make no junk. We need to understand the awesome responsibility put upon us. He's given us to be stewards of these earthly vessels and we need to embrace that responsibility with all the passion we can. Stop allowing others to tell you who and what you are. How you're supposed to look and how you're supposed to feel. The only person you need to please is Him. Walk according to the precepts and examples He has set. You were made in His image; act like it.

So, now let's get back Solomon's idea that we are like rubies. You may wonder can rubies be man-made. Yes, in a nutshell, rubies can be synthetically made. But a good woman can only be made by God. That's why you're far more precious than rubies. It's time for you to align your view of yourself, with God's view of you. To obtain this strength you must come to Christ by faith.

You may ask, "How do I do that?" Well for me, I had to remember my union with God. The Message Bible says, in 1Corinthians 15:10, that because God was so gracious, so very generous, here I am. And I'm not about to let His grace go to waste. Haven't I worked hard trying to do more than any of the others? Even then, my work didn't amount to all that much. It was God, giving me the work to do; God giving me the energy to do it. Cheryl is nothing without Him. Everything I touch would fail, but because I have a personal relationship with God, I've been able to move forward from my despair. Next, I had to consider the work of My Father in heaven. Look at Philipiansl 2:13 which says this.

What I'm getting at, friends, is that you should simply keep on doing what you've done from the beginning. "When I was living among you, you lived in responsive obedience. Now that I'm separated from you, keep it up. Better yet, redouble your efforts. Be energetic in your life of salvation, reverent and sensitive before God." Phillipians 2:12 That energy is God's energy; energy deep within you; God, Himself, willing and working at what will give Him the most pleasure. For its God, who works in you, to will and to act according to His good purpose. Whenever life got in the way, I never gave up. I increased my efforts. When one door closed, I just went to the next one, fully expecting that when I got to the right one, God would open it up and pour me out a blessing that I wouldn't have room for. God honored that in me.

I depended on my source of supply and recognized my potential for fruitfulness.

God says, "I am the Vine, you are the branches. When you're joined with me and I with you, the relation is intimate and organic, the harvest is sure to be abundant. Separated, you can't produce a thing. Anyone who separates from me is deadwood, gathered up and thrown on the bonfire. But if you make yourselves at home with me and my words are at home in you, you can be sure that whatever you ask will be listened to and acted upon." This is how my Father shows who he is—when you produce grapes, when you mature as my disciples. John 15 4-5.

God works through people, but He is your ultimate source. I couldn't listen to the naysayers and those who had doomed me before I even started. The God, in me was greater than the whole world, and He proves it each and every day. My God is enabling and I had to affirm that. God didn't give us a spirit of fear, but a spirit of power, of love and of a sound mind 2 Timothy 1:7.

I was like Paul; I waited on God to judge me. It mattered, very little to me, what anybody thought of me; even less, where I ranked in popular opinion. I still don't even rank myself, because comparisons, in these matters are pointless. I'm not aware of anything that would disqualify me from being a good guide for you, but that doesn't mean much. The Master makes that judgment. I only focus on God's view of me and not even my own.

The royal ruby gem has fascinated people in the past and entrances people in the present. Rubies will only continue to mesmerize people for many years to come. Thus, rubies make for an excellent and timeless addition to your jewelry collection. And a good woman, a worthy and virtuous woman, will make a timeless addition to the kingdom of God.

Peace in the Storm

*A*nd when he was entered into a ship, his disciples followed him. And, behold, there arose a great tempest in the sea, insomuch that the ship was covered with the waves: but he was asleep. And his disciples came to him, and awoke him, saying, Lord, save us: we perish. And he saith unto them, Why are ye fearful, O ye of little faith? Then he arose, and rebuked the winds and the sea; and there was a great calm. Matthew 8:23-26.

There was a knock at the door. It was the postman with a piece of certified mail from the Tax Assessor's Office. I remember thinking what could this be about. I opened the letter, and to my surprise, it threatened to evict me from my home if I didn't pay the requested amount. This was my first home and it was owner-financed. The previous owner never told me, so I had no idea I was supposed to pay property taxes. Not only had he not given me this information, he owed for two years of back taxes on the home as well. Imagine the dismay, the outrage, and the confusion I endured. I had been trying to do the right thing; it was all I could do to make the monthly payments. I was already struggling and robbing Peter to pay Paul. How was I ever going to come up with the amount of money I needed to keep them from taking my home?

Storms are a necessary part of our journey. The Bible says in this life we will have tribulation. It goes on to say the rain falls on the 'just' and the 'unjust' and a man's days upon the earth are few and full of trouble. Difficulties, troubles, trials, hard times, and problems, will come; but Jesus reminds us to be of good cheer for He has overcome the world. Knowing trouble to be a reality; "Are you ready for the storm?"

Clouds will gather, the wind will blow, and the storms will rage because nothing in life was meant to come easy. A good marriage, a family that stays together, and children that grow up to love the Lord, require an investment of your time if you expect a good return.

Women, What the Hell are You Thinking Now?

With over fifty percent of marriages failing today, maintaining a marriage of purpose is difficult at best. But there's a God that wants to be at the very center of your marriage relationship to help you if you'll let him.

Pants hanging to their knees, skirts to their thighs, television messages of violence, and disrespect; if we want children who serve the Lord we must fight for them to save them from this godless and perverse society. But there is a God that wants to help you as mothers train your child in the way they should go.

Fighting the good fight of faith and being ready for the storms of life is your only saving grace. The adversary wants to do you in and destroy you. He's against you and doesn't want you to live a life of victory. But God is raising up a standard against the enemy. He's ready to use you today. But, "Are you ready for the storm?" 1 Peter 4:12-13: Beloved, think it not strange concerning the fiery trial which is to try you, as though some strange thing happened unto you: But rejoice, inasmuch as ye are partakers of Christ's sufferings; that, when his glory shall be revealed, ye may be glad also with exceeding joy.

The book of Isaiah says that sometimes God has to give us the bread of affliction and the water of adversity for a little while. It says he's trying to show us the right way to go. His voice is telling us, "This is the way. Don't go to the left and don't go to the right; but this is the way straight ahead."

2 Corinthians 4:15-18: For all things are for your sakes, that the abundant grace might through the thanksgiving of many resound to the glory of God For which cause we faint not; but though our outward man perish, yet the inward man is renewed day by day. For our light affliction, which is but for a moment, worketh for us a far more exceeding and eternal weight of glory. While we look not at the things which are seen, but at the things which are not seen: for the things which are seen are temporal; but the things which are not seen are eternal.

The sky is blue, sunlight is piercing through the morning dew and you're sailing along with perfect weather on calm serene seas; and all of a sudden, "POW," the storm hits. Your spouse decides after years of marriage they no longer want to be with you. Your child ends up in jail because they've been indulging in illicit activity. You arrive at your home only to find out it won't be your home any longer because you're being evicted.

Have you ever felt like the disciples mentioned in our scripture felt progressing along nicely – the sun shining, the winds calm, and the water smooth – and then all of a sudden "KABOOM" the storm hits your life? When I got that letter from the tax assessor, I was taken by surprise, the breath was knocked out of me and I didn't know which way to turn. I looked up to Heaven and said "What's really going on? Why is this happening to me? Don't you care that I'm in trouble? You gave me this house as an answer to prayer and now you're gonna just let them take it away?"

Matthew 8:24 says that the ship was covered with the waves. Mark 4:37 says the waves beat into the ship. Luke 8:23 says they were filled with water and were in jeopardy. Not unlike the ship the disciples sailed in that day, the waves of adversity were beating against the sides of my life and I can't swim. I was covered with problems, storms, difficulties, and trials. Nothing was stable, nothing was grounded, everything was shaking and I was in jeopardy. I looked up once more and said, "God don't you care? Just when I'm living for you like I should, just when I'm doing the right things in my life. Why now?"

Well, I have a witness who knows a little something about storms. Job 23:8-10: Behold, I go forward, but he is not there; and backward, but I cannot perceive him: On the left hand, where he doth work, but I cannot behold him: he hideth himself on the right hand, that I cannot see him: But he knoweth the way that I take: when he hath tried me, I shall come forth as gold.

Gold is a soft metal. In order to get it to the right consistency other elements must be added. The refining process involves grinding separating and heating. Job knew to trust God. He knew through each level of the refining process, he would come through better than before despite the hell being allowed to infiltrate his life. We too must be processed and refined, ground down to our core in order to be separated from the world, and heated by the Spirit of God; so that in the end we'll come forth as pure gold.

What about Abraham; his whole life was a trial. Genesis 22:11-14: And the angel of the LORD called unto him out of heaven, and said, Abraham, Abraham: and he said, "Here am I". And he said, "Lay not thine hand upon the lad, neither do thou anything unto him: for now I know that thou fearest God, seeing thou hast not withheld thy son, thine only son from me." And Abraham lifted up his eyes, and looked, and behold behind him a ram caught in a thicket by his horns: and Abraham went and took the ram, and offered him up for a burnt offering in the stead of his son. And Abraham called the name of that place Jehovah jireh: as it is said to this day, in the mount of the LORD it shall be seen. God provided a ram in the bush just in the nick of time. David went through trials, Moses had storms in his life, Elijah had difficult times, Jacob faced adversity, Peter was tried, Joseph had his share of hard times, Daniel had the lion's den, the three Hebrew boys had the fiery furnace, and Jesus had a cross and a lost world. There's no doubt about it, there will be storms in your life. They'll rock you, shake you, test your faith and bring adversity. But the storm won't last forever. As real as your pain is right now, it will be gone one day. As deep as your despair may reside, as unrelenting as the heartache may appear to be, it'll all be taken care of one day.

Romans 8:31-39: What shall we then say to these things? If God be for us, who can be against us? He that spared not his own Son, but delivered him up for us all, how shall he not with him also freely give us all things? Who shall lay anything to the charge of God's elect? It is God that justifieth. Who is he that condemneth? It is Christ that died, yea rather, that is risen again, who is even at the right hand of God, who also maketh intercession for us. Who shall separate us from the love of Christ? Shall tribulation, or distress, or persecution, or famine, or nakedness, or peril, or sword? As it is written, for thy sake we are killed all the day long; we are accounted as sheep for the slaughter. Nay, in all these things we are more than conquerors through him that loved us. For I am persuaded, that neither death, nor life, nor angels, nor principalities, nor powers, nor things present, nor things to come, nor height, nor depth, nor any other creature, shall be able to separate us from the love of God, which is in Christ Jesus our Lord. If God be for us who can be against us? Who shall lay anything to the charge of God's elect?

Who is He that condemns? Who shall separate us from the love of God? Command your problem to come under submission to the Almighty God. Declare any weapon secretly fashioned against you will die in the name of Jesus. Declare peace to be still right now!

STRENGTH FOR THE STRUGGLE

"Apart from me, you can do nothing. John 15:5. Amazingly wonderful things can happen when you're blessed with a strong-willed personality like mine. But I hadn't matured enough to allow the Holy Spirit to be in control. As a confident, demanding, purposeful woman, I struggled to let go of control. God wanted to teach me, so I could be blessed by Him. But as a woman with a will of iron, I thought fast, moved fast, made decisions fast, and expected others to do the same. I had the single-minded, focused, mentality most women have particularly after a less-than-amicable divorce. I was an independent, take charge, woman; persistent and resolute. But none of that matters if you're not being led by God.

I was raised in a family of two girls. My mother's constant admonition was, "Do well in school so you'll be able to take care of yourself." This was so important to our mother that many times my sister and I were excused from chores so we could have time to study. Compelled by the insistence of our mother, my sister and I both were excellent scholars. We attended schools for the gifted and talented and in my high school years I attended a school geared toward the medical profession. My life had been mapped out, prearranged, set on course. But there was something missing. No one had factored God's plan for my life into the equation. Everyone was deciding the schools I would attend, what profession I should be in, and all the perks success would bring. When I became pregnant at sixteen all those plans were aborted. In our minds we believed everything-all the hopes, all the dreams, all the aspirations of greatness-- were destroyed. But it wasn't our job to decide.

Even through the domestic violence I suffered at the hands of my ex-husband, God's providence was already at work and He had mapped out a plan for me, just as He has for everyone else. God was at work through my circumstances, developing my testimony, and showing me how to overcome. He was laying the foundation for my deliverance. He was inviting me to be involved with Him in His works with the people of God. In all things, He gets the glory. How I viewed the trials, tribulations, and inconveniences of life formed the basis for my future. Rather than seeing them as road blocks, I saw them as springboards for promotion, or character developers and these personal thoughts became my personal reality. God's invitation to me to work with Him was a defining moment that involved the crises of domestic violence, single parenting, and my response required both faith and action on my part. I could either choose to accept it and be covered by His mercy and grace, or go at it on my own and wander aimlessly for the rest of my life. The Word tells us His plans for us are plans of good and not of evil to give us a future and a hope. Our lives are ultimately about much more than the superficial influences around us. I was at a defining moment in my life; would I be the instrument through whom God would speak, or would I miss His will for my life and sink into self-pity and despair about my situation?

Educated, made my own way; pulled myself up by my bootstraps--that was my mind set--yet I still felt a void. I was still empty inside. Truthfully, without God, none of us would be anything. God's definition of success is very different from our own.

We are God's representatives here on earth. Our ultimate success in life comes from knowing His will for us and pursuing it. In the last days you won't be judged by how much money you have, or the clothes you wear, or the car you drive. Only what you do for Christ will last.

So, I ask how many people have you helped along the way? To whom have you given your support morally, financially, emotionally, or spiritually? When Jesus was asked which commandments were the greatest, he replied: to love the Lord your God completely and to love your neighbor as yourself. Have you tried it--loving your neighbor I mean? Or do you believe that it's every man for himself?

How would you assess you faith and love, your attitudes, your responses to life, your talk, your interests, the way you invest and spend your time, your mindset and use of money? Positive attitudes and a mature personality are rarely present in individuals who believe they alone are responsible for their success. Out of balance, we become unrealistic about our abilities. Unable to face facts about ourselves and our lives, we see things through rose-colored glasses. Our drive causes us to be hard, unbending, production oriented, women. Persistence makes us indifferent and obstinate, responding immaturely to people about our situations.

Women, What the Hell are You Thinking Now?

Pessimistic outlooks, emphasis on materialism, inclinations to instant gratification rather than obedience, all lead us to fall off course with relation to God's plan for our lives. Increasing the intake of the Word through the unction of the Spirit will move us in the right direction. God has a purpose and it will be revealed in His way and in His time. God is setting out to accomplish His purposes and He is looking for people, women, that will not avoid their assignment because they're afraid of the trials they may face regardless of how challenging, costly, or demanding they may be. Believing in God's providential plan for my life, teen parenting, domestic violence, single motherhood, all placed me in position to be a living testimony to God's goodness and mercy. His grace was sufficient for me. I was not in those situations by accident or mistake. I was there by divine providence for a divine purpose. As people see now how God has delivered me through the trials of life, He deserves all the glory. My struggles have not been about me. He chose me so I could strengthen others experiencing the same conditions. I now speak to you as one with a testimony glorifying God for strength through the struggle.

Knowing how to discern God's will for your life isn't a mystery. Study the Word and meditate on it day and night. Through His Word, God will reveal Himself to you and you can be assured He will never go contrary to what

His Word reveals. Know that because we want something badly, doesn't mean it's God's plan for our lives. Everything good to us, isn't good for us. We have to stop convincing ourselves that its God's will when it really isn't. Costly obedience is often required. Don't pamper the flesh and let your emotions control you. If that man is not your husband and He insists on having sex with you outside of marriage, he's not in the will of God. Therefore, he's not for you if you're a woman seeking God's will for your life. Feeling God failed you because He didn't answer your prayers the way you expected, or believing he dealt you a low blow because of the way He made you, or the parents He gave you, or the environment you grew up in, only leads you to believe you're at the helm of your own ship. Expecting more from others than they're willing to give, getting your eyes off God and onto others, and expecting from them what only God can give, pushes you further into self- absorption.

Refusing to read and live the Word daily, you'll find yourself caught up in situations of your own making that are difficult to get out of and it's futile to blame God for the problem. Many times that's the real issue. We don't want to know God's true will for our lives, because then we're held accountable and must take responsibility for our own actions and disobedience enduring the consequences in the long run. Ultimately, we find we are disappointed in ourselves and

Women, What the Hell are You Thinking Now?

because we can't accept ourselves the way we are, we set up walls of bitterness and resentment between God and us, and between other people and ourselves.

Only those whose purpose it is to know God's specific plan for their lives will find it. He doesn't reveal it to us so we can consider it or compare it to our own. He reveals it, so we can do it. What kind of assignment is God preparing you for? Prepare yourself for your defining moment. Obey God's voice in whatever He asks; whatever the cost may be.

A Rock in a Hard Place

And the LORD said, Behold, there is a place by me, and thou shalt stand upon a rock. Exodus 33:21.

For me, marriage seemed to be the right thing to do. After all, we already had a child. But life has a way of shaking marriages; Domestic violence, financial difficulties, and lack of communication to name a few. The marriage crumbled, the relationship deteriorated, and before long I was staring at the papers that said, 'Divorce Granted.'

Drowning in the depths of deception, adrift in moral chaos, our world is deteriorating fast. At an ever increasing pace, our world is changing the rules. Sin is no longer sin. Wrong is no longer wrong. Self- gratifying as our society is, the prevailing idea is to do whatever pleases you. Looking for solid ground or a place of safety in immoral relationships, alcohol, drugs, working as if there's no tomorrow, and material things; we slip further into ourselves with no hope for recovery. Faith simply can't be found in this world because things are constantly shifting back and forth. Our world in its present state is sitting on sinking sand. But there's a rock in a hard place. There's a place we can find that will shelter us during the storms of life. On the rock there's: security, safety, healing, comfort, peace, and shelter in the storms of life. On Christ the solid rock I stand, all other ground is sinking sand.

I walked into the clinic offices on a Friday afternoon only to be told that I was being let go due to job abandonment. "How could that be? I had a note from one of your doctors explaining my son has chicken pox? You even saw him with your own eyes. Besides I had vacation time and took it! How can you do this to me after five years?" I was devastated. I had been a good employee for five years. Why would they treat me this way? "What do I do now? Where do I turn? Who'll take care of us?"

There's a rock in a hard place.

How many times have we heard the words, "We have to lay you off, I want a divorce, it's cancer, your loved one or best friend has passed away, there's been an accident?" Maybe I haven't described your situation or the exact words, but the pain you've felt from words just like these have torn through the seams of your existence and ripped apart the fabric of your life; but I want you to know there's a rock in a hard place.

Luke 6:46-49 reminds us not to pretend to serve God with our lips and not our heart. He tells us not to put on a show in church and then act differently everywhere else. He lets us know if we're not willing to do what God says, then our labor is in vain.

God said, "I would rather you be stone cold than for you to fake it." He said, "I would rather that you were either hot or cold but if you're lukewarm, I will spit you out of my mouth." He says, he that hears me and does what I say - he is like a man that builds on a solid foundation. But he that hears me and doesn't do what I say - he is like one building with no foundation."

In this same scripture the floods came to both houses. The storms rose up upon both houses. The rains beat upon both houses. The winds blew against both houses. But it was only the house built upon the rock that was able to stand.

I'm talking to people who've gone through some something's, people who've experienced storms in their lives. You've had to face pressures that you thought would cause you to be crushed. You've endured what you perceive as one never-ending night in your life and you've wondered if daylight will ever dawn again. Just when it seems you're getting to your feet something else knocks you down; financial pressure, family pressure, marital pressure, job pressure, you feel the squeeze that life's placed on you. It's a hard place but I want you to know there is a rock in a hard place.

When I walked out of that clinic after being employed there for over five years I was hurt, confused, and despondent. But I held on to the fact God had always been with me and if my season there was up; there would be a new place for me to grow. Despite the blowing wind, the beating rain, and the rolling waters of the floods trying to wash my life away; I waited to be planted in my new field.

For some of you it's been a difficult time. So, I can't tell you how to build your life so you don't have to face the storms; there's no way to insulate yourself so you don't have any problems. But I can tell you how to fortify your thinking so you can have a firm foundation on which to stand as you hunker down and ride out the storms. Enduring the storms of life begins by digging deep and setting your foundation on the rock that is Jesus the Christ!

You see, the devil wants you to get you so wrapped up in the storm that you miss the revival that God has for

Women, What the Hell are You Thinking Now?

your life. He wants you so afraid of the winds, that you miss the blessing. But you need to resist the devil and tell him, "I have a rock in a hard place and no matter what you throw my way, I'm standing on that firm foundation."

Psalm 15 tells us how to get on the rock. It reminds us in the time of trouble, He'll hide us in His pavilion: in the secret of His tabernacle, set us on a rock.

I applied for position after position; only to be turned down. Then out of nowhere, I got a call from a school. They wanted me to come in to interview for a position as an instructor. "Instructor," I thought. I've never done that before in my life." But I went anyway. I got the job on the spot. As I left, I remembered all the dreams I'd had of speaking before people and I thought, "How awesome is our God. He knows His plans for us even if we don't and His will be done." That job led me to where I am today-- traveling the country speaking before thousands of people. Something I never would've done had I stayed at the clinic. God moved me for a purpose; because all things work together for the good of those who love the Lord and are called according to His purpose. What I thought was a setback (losing my job), was a set-up for a comeback (speaking before thousands of people). I no longer look at things through my mind's eye; I try to see them through God's eyes because His thoughts are not my thoughts, and

CHERYL LACEY DONOVAN

His ways are not my ways. He knows what's best and when you trust Him, truly trust Him; He'll deliver on His promises. There is a rock in a hard place.

CRUSHED BUT NOT BROKEN

But we have this treasure in earthen vessels that the excellency of the power may be of God, and not of us. We are troubled on every side, yet not distressed; we are perplexed, but not in despair; Persecuted, but not forsaken; cast down, but not destroyed; Always bearing about in the body the dying of the Lord Jesus, that the life also of Jesus might be made manifest in our body. For we who live are always delivered unto death for Jesus' sake, that the life also of Jesus might be made manifest in our mortal flesh. So then death worketh in us, but life in you. 2 Corinthians 4:7-12.

I had always heard the army was no place for a black man. I must concur. I will always believe in my heart the

Army changes people. My husband was no exception. Somehow he disappeared into the rank and file that was called the Army. All the stories of, "Be all you can be," only apply to certain people. The Army may be the place where boys go to become men, but what kind of men do they become?

One evening my husband invited some of his Army buddies to our home. We sat and chatted about various and sundry things. The time went by almost in obscurity. Surprisingly, when our guests left, my husband began ranting and raving about how I was trying to entice the men he had invited over. Confused and amazed, I started thinking about how just a few months earlier; I was flattered he wanted me all to himself.

My husband had never behaved this way before. The entire night he kept screaming about how my leg shook back and forth in a tantalizing motion. He believed this was some sort of invitation for sex. I was very pregnant. I didn't even want him. How could he believe I wanted someone else?

The argument quickly escalated into one of physical confrontation; first a push, then a shove, and before long a slap to the face that left me stunned and in shock. The sting from the open handed lick, he had inflicted, felt like a million ants biting me at one time. I didn't know whether to run or cry. I did both.

Women, What the Hell are You Thinking Now?

Running up the stairs, my husband giving chase the entire way, I was afraid of what he might do if he caught me. I was even more afraid for my unborn child. I locked myself in my oldest son's room. I sat on the bed holding him as I listened to his father frantically trying to open the door. Being physical was not something I was accustomed to. Even as a child I rarely experienced any form of physical punishment.

Proceeding to grab me and push me to the floor, my husband injured my soul more than he injured my body. Knowing that my father never beat me, I resolved neither would my husband. Fighting back with everything I had in me, pregnancy was the last thing on my mind. This was the first physical attack I could remember, but it was definitely not the last. My husband had been drinking and using drugs prior to the altercation. I had no idea.

The next day I awoke to, "I'm sorry. You know I love you right? You know I didn't mean to hurt you. You're my Babe." Becoming the endearing, charming, loving man that I had married, complete with flowers and dinner, he was very apologetic about the whole ordeal. So the cycle began and continued even into our separation and impending divorce.

Disheveled, heartbroken, and disillusioned, I called my mother at work.

"Mama?" I cried.

"Yes, Cheryl, what's wrong?" As a minister of motherhood, my mother immediately knew something was wrong.

"Something bad happened, Mama," I expelled between sniffles and tears. "Something really bad, please come home."

"What happened, Cheryl?" she yelled and questioned frantically.

"Mom, just come home, please," I muffled, barely able to get the sentence from my mind to my tongue.

"Cheryl!" she screamed.

I hung up the phone.

A friend of mine, concerned that I had not shown up for work, called me. When I told her what had happened, she too rushed to be by my side. Within the hour, both my Mother and my friend were at the house. As my Mother approached me, I lowered my head in shame. Her strong hands, grabbed me by my face, and demanded I tell her what happened to me. Her tear-filled eyes, scanned me from top to bottom, and with each stare, she became more saddened.

"Why are your clothes torn, Cheryl?" she asked. "What happened?"

Sadness consumed me, and I began to feel weak. As tears flooded my eyes, and poured profusely from my face, I lifted my head, and with despair, I stared back at my Mother, and revealed to her, the suffering I endured at the hands of her son-in-law.

"I dropped the children off. And..."

"And, what, Cheryl?" she demanded.

"He said you were on the phone..."

"I would never call you there. Oh God, what happened, Cheryl? What did he do to you!" she yelled a loud and thunderous moan.

I felt her soul aching.

"He raped me, Mama."

It was at this time my foundation, rooted in the word of God, had been shattered. I was trying to do right, yet, I was being knocked down at every turn; for a split-second, I questioned God and His motives and His power.

One of the largest battles of my life would be to discover how was I ever to trust another man again? How would I ever be able to have intimate feelings again? How could I trust even my own judgment?

The destructive actions of abuse and its messages threatened to bind me. The guilt and shame that I felt engulfed me like a flame. I struggled not to internalize the destructive messages so that I wouldn't end up in a place that God didn't intend for my life. Internalizing the violence, caused self-blame rather than the ability to see myself in the process of becoming.

You see, you struggle every day to hold on to a little piece of your soul so that it doesn't end up slipping away completely. My children were a large part of that. God, through the love of my children, convinced me to leave my troubles with Him. That moment I questioned God, was traded for a lifetime of devotion to Him. God taught me, LOVE DOESN'T HURT! Instead, Corinthians offers us a description of love that says its kind and long-suffering, it bears all things, and believes all things. God didn't create you to be dominated. You were created in His image therefore no one has the right to violate your body, your mind, or your soul in ways that cause you to be wounded emotionally, spiritually or physically. And for those of you who believe that you can't leave for fear of financial ruin, or being alone to raise children, "God has NOT given you the spirit of fear; but of love, power, and a sound mind" (2 Timothy 1:7.). You can do all things through Christ that strengthens you (Philippians 4:13).

Believing you can't make it on your own is a lie of the enemy. Don't give into it. In 2 Corinthians 4:7-10, the Apostle Paul sums up our existence on earth; His analogy is that we're in a pressure cooker! The challenges of life and the stresses they cause are constant companions. But, while

Women, What the Hell are You Thinking Now?

we share in the same troubles that the world has, God has assured us we will overcome! Paul says it this way, "We are pressed on all sides, but not crushed!"

Paul understands that living in this world, we will have trouble. In fact, the Bible promises it, "Man that is born of a woman is of few days, and full of trouble." Job 14:1. Jesus even promised it! "In the world ye shall have tribulation..." John 16:33. But, God also promises He will surely deliver you from your troubles.

"Surely, He shall deliver thee from the snare of the fowler," Psalm. 91:1-3. Thank God, we have His promise of delivery. "Many are the afflictions of the righteous, but God delivereth him out of them all!" We may be pressed on all sides but we won't be crushed!

The good news is you'll not only come through, but you'll be better than before.

It may sound strange now, but I thank God every day for my ex-husband because he taught me many things. Not the kind of lessons you can learn in a classroom or in Sunday school, but lessons that can only come from experience, wisdom, and maturity. Without him, I may never have learned how resilient I could truly be. I wouldn't know the true meaning of forgiveness.

But don't just take my word for it. Let's ask some witnesses in the Bible. What about Job? Reading about his life can be depressing. Disease, death, poverty, and loss of support from loved ones all pressed him down. But you can't stop there. You have to read the rest of the story…Job 42:10-12 says, "So the Lord blessed the later end of Job more than his beginning!"

Is there anyone out there who wants their latter days to be better than their former days; who wants their end to be better than their beginning, their future to be better than their past?

What about Joseph? Forsaken and falsely accused by family and friends, he was left in a pit to die and ultimately taken into captivity. But, he kept the right attitude. He kept the right perspective when he told his brothers, in Genesis 50:20, "Ye thought evil against me; but God meant it unto good!"

The Apostle Paul said it right, "we are pressed on all sides, but not crushed!" You can't keep a child of the kingdom down! Surely, you'll come out of your troubles better than before! We may get knocked down by troubles, but, thank God we don't get knocked out.

Tough situations remind us to put all our trust in God, because the Word of God says the righteous shall be victorious. God uses suffering to help us grow spiritually. Without problems we can become selfish, spoiled, and self-sufficient. Adversity is a wake-up call that draws us closer to

Him. Every now and then, we will suffer affliction, but God is faithful; and He will keep us from being crushed or beaten down! Everything, even our struggles are for His glory. Because most of us live much of our lives under a cloud of self-deception thinking more highly of ourselves than we ought, we fail to realize suffering can also help us gain an accurate perspective about ourselves. God can sometime test us and put us through trials to draw out what's truly in our hearts. It's when problems arise that we must face our lack of faith, our self- centeredness, our suppressed hostilities, and our weaknesses. We may be perplexed or have questions about why God is allowing these things to happen to us, but God can give us the strength not to be controlled by the circumstance because ultimately, He is always in control. We may be persecuted, misused, abused, lied on, and cheated - but because of Him, we can rest on the knowledge that we won't be forsaken, because He has never forsaken the righteous. We could be knocked down, but God will keep us from being destroyed.

Trust in the Lord with all your heart and lean not to your own understanding. In all your ways acknowledge Him and He shall direct your path.

God has proven time and time again He can be trusted. I trust in Him with every fiber of my being. So I now encourage you to let go of the situation and let Him be God for a little while.

It's time to admit it – most of the times when pressed down and perplexed, you don't have a clue what's going on. We like to think that we do because we want to have some sense of control but God's desire for us is to come to a place of total surrender and allow Him to rule supreme in our lives. Seeing God in your circumstances is the key to victory. Wanting to grow mature and become better than your adversity will only occur when you learn to see God behind every issue of life and He has something good for you in the problem. Trusting Him in all circumstances helps you to learn all He's trying to teach you, receiving all He's trying to give you and growing in a way He's trying to grow you. Refusing to trust Him will cause you to miss what He's trying to accomplish in you through the pain.

The passage of the virtuous woman teaches us that virtuous women are industrious, good managers, providers and above all else they are faithful to God. Every human life is the reflection of God. He created us in His own image. Wives (not those shacking or otherwise with a significant other), the Bible does tell you to be submissive to your husbands. Wives, submit to your own husbands, as to the Lord. For the husband is head of the wife, as also Christ is head of the church; and He is the Savior of the body. Therefore, just as the church is subject to Christ, so let the wives be to their own husbands in everything. Ephesians 5: 22-24. But nowhere is it written that you should be his punching bag. Nor is it written that you should be demeaned and belittled with words. Instead the bible gives specific conditions as to how your husband should interact with you in order for you to be submissive to him. Husbands, love your wives, just as Christ also loved the church and gave Himself for her, that He might sanctify and cleanse her with the washing of water by the Word, that He might present her to Himself, a glorious church, not having spot or wrinkle or any such thing, but that she should be holy and without blemish. So husbands ought to love their own wives as their own bodies; he who loves his wife, loves himself. For no one ever hated his own flesh, but nourishes and cherishes it, just as the Lord does the church. Ephesians 5: 25-29, "Instead, whoever wants to become great among you must be your servant, and whoever wants to be first, must be your slave -- just as the Son of Man did not come to be served, but to serve, and to give His life as a ransom for many," Matthew 20:26 28.

  Jesus' entire existence here on earth was about servant leadership. The way your husband: loves you, protects you, provides for you, and cares for you should exemplify all of the principles left by Christ. He shouldn't neglect, ignore, demean or abuse you. He shouldn't be rude or disrespectful. He shouldn't be arrogant or insensitive. And he shouldn't criticize you or make you feel you aren't valuable. To love and to cherish; that's what the wedding vows say. God gives the husband a position of leadership in relationship to his wife. He also requires the price of self-sacrifice from Him, and that's exactly what you should feel from your husband when he has submitted himself wholly and fully to God.

Husbands have been called to lead, not to control. They shouldn't use their role for selfish benefit. Instead their role of leadership should be one of service. Deviating from the purpose of God's headship because of abuse and mistreatment causes them to lose God's endorsement. This is the fatal mistake many husbands make when they try to brow beat their wives into submission. God has attached strings to the leadership role of husbands in a marriage, but some allow their motives for leading a marriage spiritually to become mixed with selfish gain.

God doesn't want you to stay in an abusive situation. Understand a lot of the pain we suffer in life is a direct result of our own choices. We can choose our choices, but we can't choose the consequences. Love is not equivalent to violence. The fruits of the spirit include love and kindness (Galatians

5:22), not abuse and violence. If you are an abused women, you need to learn to say no, set boundaries, and protect yourself. You also need to learn that you deserve to be treated with respect (Proverbs 31:25, 28). You don't need to tolerate abuse. If you are unequally yoked, the Bible says, "Now in a like exchange--I speak as to children--open wide to us also. Do not be bound together with unbelievers; for what partnerships have righteousness and lawlessness, or what fellowship has light with darkness? Or what harmony has Christ with Belial, or what has a believer in common with an unbeliever?" 2 Corinthians 6 13-15. You should go to God in prayer and ask for His guidance in your situation, but remember, you need to be prepared for the answer and know that when He answers you, He has already made provisions to take care of you.

    Remember in the Book of Daniel chapter 3; we see where Three Hebrew children acknowledged God. They didn't compromise their belief by bowing to a foreign god. As a result, they were bound and cast into a fiery furnace. But the King didn't see three men bound being consumed by fire, he saw four men loosed and walking around. They came out without a burn mark on them, and they didn't even smell like smoke. Three chapters later we see where Daniel found himself in a situation where he didn't even think twice about acknowledging God. As a result, Daniel ended up in a den of lions.

In the 16th chapter of Acts we find Paul and Silas in jail. But instead of groaning and complaining about their circumstances, they began to acknowledge God. They begin praying, singing and shouting praises unto the Lord. And when they did, the ground began to shake, the earth began to quake, and the chains and prison doors that held them captive swung wide open.

In each of these situations, God miraculously paved a divine pathway just as He did for me. When you acknowledge God, He will: stand with you in the midst of a fiery furnace, shut the mouths of ravenous lions, and break the chains of bondage, and open doors that hold you captive. He will deliver you from an abusive marriage and see too it you and your children are provided for.

If you're at your wits end and don't know which way to turn trust God – completely and totally, don't try to figure it out for yourself. Acknowledge Him in every aspect of your life and allow Him to direct your steps .They that wait upon the Lord shall renew their strength; they shall mount up with wings as eagles; they shall run, and not be weary; and they shall walk, and not faint. God is at work in your life - even when you don't recognize it or understand it. He's in the storm with you. He's calling you to rise above it.

Women, What the Hell are You Thinking Now?

Keep your eyes on Him during the storm so it doesn't get you down!

"Blessed is the man that endureth trouble: for when he is tried, he shall receive the crown of life." Those who go through fire should remember its God's way of refining and cleansing you for your good and His glory. Trouble is simply the factory God is using to manufacture the right type of product in our lives.

Press toward the Mark

Philippians 3:13, "Brethren, I count not myself to have apprehended: but this one thing I do, forgetting those things which are behind, and reaching forth unto those things which are before I press toward the mark of the high calling in Christ Jesus."

Have you suffered abuse; abuse occurring at the hands of a mother, father, sister, brother, or family member. Abuse can range from being physically punched, to being called out of your name by someone you love. This includes parents. "Sticks and stones may break your bones and words do hurt you in ways that people may never know." No one in your family has a right to abuse you verbally, physically, emotionally, sexually, psychologically, or otherwise; not even your parents. Fathers, provoke not your children to anger, lest they be discouraged. (Colossians 3:21). Furthermore, the theory about sparing the rod and spoiling the child did not include beatings with extensions cords, broom handles, or water hoses. God does not chastise his children in such a way as to mutilate, humiliate or totally destroy them. Parents shouldn't do it either. Do you feel that you were treated differently, not necessarily abusively, but differently, from your siblings as a child? Guess what, you should have been. You are an individual, not a clone of your sibling. Therefore, your relationship with your parents should have been different from that of your sibling. Surprise! If you have feelings of anger, rage, bitterness and un-forgiveness lingering in your heart as a result of what you perceive to be past abuses, know that Christ can heal you, but He is a gentleman and He will only do what you invite Him to do. When you are a believer in Jesus Christ, His Holy Spirit can help you to live life according to God's perfect plan.

    One thing the enemy doesn't want us to do is forget about our past, or forget about the ones who hurt us, or disappointed us. The reason he continues to replay this as if it's happening right before your eyes, is because he knows you won't only let him play it, but he can bring up old feelings that you thought you were delivered from, and before you know it, you got an attitude, you're yelling at your children, you're disrespectful to your husband, some of us even start cussing, or want to fight. We indulge in anything and everything that's opposite of what God tells us to do.

Let me help free somebody.

The devil only has the power that you give him. You can speak death or you can speak life. The enemy tries you when you are weak and vulnerable, he doesn't come near you when your mind is on God and you're in your Word; but he patiently waits until you slip up, and then he comes at you with everything he has because you use to be in his kingdom on his side, and now you're in God's kingdom, so he has to pull out all the stops to get you back.

There's only two reasons the devil won't attack: 1) H already has you, or 2) You don't have anything he wants. Either way, check your walk with God. All those generational curses that have passed down from family member to family member can end with you. You can speak it declare it and believe it in the name of Jesus. You can stop thinking about what's happened to you, and start thanking God for His mercy and grace. You're giving too much power to people; allowing them to decide if and when they want to be your friend, allowing them to tell you what your calling is, even though you know they're way off, allowing them to speak into your life things not of God allowing them to decide how they're going to treat you, allowing people to use you with their money.

But it's about getting free. See I have no problem being transparent about my life; don't judge a book by its cover, just because I'm blessed and anointed; I go through trials and tribulations just like everybody else. God showed me the strongholds that not only the devil, but people had on me. When God opened my eyes, the devil knew he was in trouble. I was no longer walking around in my wilderness, I'm not only free from the bondage of the enemy, I'm free from people. I have a different attitude now about what you think about me, it really doesn't matter, because I know what the Father thinks about me.

It's imperative that you deal with the issues of your past, If you don't they'll continue to control you in some way. Your present, and your future, depend on your ability to move on from being an angry, bitter, resentful child, and blossoming into a mature, spirit-filled woman of God. The only person that these negative feelings will be hurting is you. Speak to someone qualified to help you work through your negative thoughts and feelings. Once you have released them, you will be free to forgive and grow spiritually. Only then, can God heal you completely. Forgiving others and releasing anger, reconnects you with God and makes it possible for Him to guide you. "In this greatly rejoice, though for a little while you may have had to suffer grief in all kinds of trials. These have come so that your faith –of greater worth than gold, which perishes even though refined by fire— may be proven genuine and may result in praise, glory, and honor when Jesus Christ is revealed."(I Peter 1:6-7).

How does one come back from such trauma and forgive? It isn't easy, but I heard someone say that being unable to forgive is like drinking poison and expecting someone else to die. Not forgiving only hurts you. Usually the perpetrator has long since moved on. You, the victim, are left to become bitter, vengeful, and resentful. If you're not careful, you'll find yourself all alone as people slowly move away because of your constant inability to maintain healthy relationships.

Consciously deciding to forgive my ex-husband for the atrocities committed against me left some people wondering if I had lost my mind. Even now, some people don't understand it. They don't really comprehend that had I not chosen to forgive my life would be on a downward spiral. Forgiveness is a mandate from God. Prayers can be hindered when one chooses to harbor un-forgiveness in their heart. I needed a breakthrough. I needed a blessing. And that blessing, that breakthrough could only come once true forgiveness entered my heart.

Let me make it clear, I didn't forget what my husband did to me; nor did I deny his responsibility. I simply chose to untie myself from the thoughts and feelings that bound me to my ex-husband's offenses. Refusing to minimize what had been done to me, I gave the hurt, shame, disappointment, and humiliation to God, and I allowed the Holy Spirit to help me forgive my ex-husband and myself. Forgiving him enriched my life in ways that no one could ever imagine. Learning to release all of the guilt, anger, bitterness, resentment, revenge and fear to God before I moved on, allowed me to let go of the past, so that I wouldn't continue to live in it. I moved into my future. And what a brilliant future it has been. Being able to recognize the kind of man I didn't want in my life was the most important lesson that my ex-husband taught me. I thank God for the wisdom I gained.

Out of all the things I've been through, I still have joy. I've been hurt, misunderstood, the devil's tried to knock me off my feet, but I'm still standing. And in the pages of this book I want to encourage each and every one of you to know that these can be your words of victory as you read these pages and face whatever comes your way. In the end of it all, you can say is, "I'm still standing!" Philippians 3:13, "Brethren, I count not myself to have apprehended: but this one thing I do, forgetting those things which are behind, and reaching forth unto those things which are before."

In verse 10 of this same passage it says, "That I may know him, and the power of his resurrection, and the fellowship of his sufferings, being made conformable unto his death." Desiring to know God and the power of His resurrection, and the fellowship of His suffering being made comfortable unto His death, Paul made a conscious choice to follow after Jesus. Desire so great, he didn't mind suffering; he didn't mind the things he had to go through, because he said in every situation I learn to be content. Paul's choice was to forget those things that were behind.

What was behind Him? People talked about him persecuted him stoned and put him in social ruin He felt the jealousy a sense of not belonging in the church because he didn't do things the way everybody else did. He was left alone, expected to die. He was tossed and driven battered by the angry sea. He was accused of all sorts of things, arrested, and beaten. But, he had a desire to know the Lord. He wanted a close relationship with God. He wanted to embrace God more than impress people. So he made up in his mind, "I'm going to forget all that stuff, I got to press toward the mark." It may not be easy, but that is my purpose. I may have to cry sometimes, but that is my goal. I may be forsaken by those that say they'll be by my side, but that's my desire. So I've got to forget all that stuff and let it go.

Moving forward the wounds of the past may appear fresh, they may even still be open, but we've got to forget it and let it go. You may have been criticized, talked about, and pushed aside because you didn't belong to the clique, or because you didn't sing so well. You may have been ostracized by the choir or the praise team, so you didn't sing anymore. Child of God your heart's desire should not be to impress man, but to embrace God. So you've got to make up in your mind, "I'm going to forget it and let it go. I may not be able to sing like an angel, but making a joyful noise unto the Lord is my desire. I must fulfill my purpose; therefore, I'm forgetting those things that are behind and I'm going to press toward the mark."

Thoughts of revenge forget it and let it go. The Lord says vengeance belongs to Him. Rejections making you feel isolated and alone forget it and let it go because the person who rejected you is a chisel in God's hand and He'll use them for your benefit. Anger due to past upsets and disappointments forget it and let it go. Feelings of depression and despair forget it and let it go.

Destiny and purpose aren't predicated on the stuff in your past. Backbiting isn't bound to your destiny. Jealousy isn't tied to your goal. Rejection can't keep you from your purpose unless you allow it to. So instead of wasting time worrying about people, instead of trying to figure out why people don't like you, instead of wondering how you can become part of the clique so you won't feel so alone, forget all that and let them go because your desire to have His promises manifested in your life as you walk in your purpose and achieve your destiny should be greater than any of that. Then and only then will God be able to use you the way He wants to. Let go of negative feelings you've been holding on to down through the years. If you want more, if you want God to use you, if you want to go to another level, you've got to do what Paul did and forget the things that are behind while pressing toward the mark for the prize of the high calling of God.

You Have to Want To

2 Kings 13:14-19.

"Now Elisha was fallen sick of his sickness whereof he died. And Joash the king of Israel came down unto him, and wept over his face, and said, O my father, my father, the chariot of Israel, and the horsemen thereof. And Elisha said unto him, Take bow and arrows. And he took unto him bow and arrows. And he said to the king of Israel; Put thine hand upon the bow. And he put his hand upon it: and Elisha put his hands upon the king's hands. And he said, Open the window eastward. And he opened it. Then Elisha said, Shoot. And he shot. And he said, The arrow of the LORD'S deliverance, and the arrow of deliverance from Syria: for thou shalt smite the Syrians in Aphek, till thou have consumed them. And he said, Take the arrows. And he took them. And he said unto the king of Israel, Smite upon the ground. And he smote thrice, and stayed. And the man of God was wroth with him, and said, Thou shouldest have smitten five or six times; then hadst thou smitten Syria till thou hadst consumed it: whereas now thou shalt smite Syria but thrice."

A murderer, an alcoholic, an adulterer, a polygamist and a prostitute, who would think God, could use any of these people? Yet, Moses killed a man, Noah was an alcoholic, David was an adulterer, Solomon was a polygamist and Mary Magdalene was a lady of the night. The good news of the gospel is, regardless of your past, all human beings are candidates for entering into the kingdom of God. Becoming a child of the King is available to everyone. Money, a theological degree from an acclaimed seminary, none of the trappings of this world is a requirement for adoption into this family. The only stipulation for entrance into the kingdom of God is you must be born again. The arms of the Lord are open to accept all who obey the gospel message. The kingdom of the Lord is different from any other. Blemishes from the past, regardless of how disreputable, aren't a deal breaker. You're given total and complete access to God, regardless of how you used to be. In the Kingdom of God, failure is not final. Instead it can be used as a stepping-stone to get to God.

David committed adultery with Bathsheba. When they learned she was pregnant with his child, he conspired to have her husband killed. But David didn't go out and hire a team of attorneys to represent him before the courts of the land. David didn't seek to defend himself. David didn't compare his transgression with others in the land. Instead he paid his dues to God and after repenting and suffering the consequences for the sin he committed, he still merited a status given to no other because after all that he was still referred to as, "A man after God's own heart." He said, "Create in me a clean heart and renew a right spirit in me, oh God. Against thee and thee only, have I sinned. Cast me not away from thy presence." David repented.

How can this be--that an adulterer who committed murder would not be restricted from the kingdom? That is the unparalleled beauty of true contrition and true repentance. When we mess up, we can get up, if we refuse to give up. Our pasts can't stop us; excuses will not exonerate us, nor can Satan keep us from finding our place. The ball lies in our court whether we'll pursue our purpose and destiny, or be pacified with the present is all up to us. How bad do you want to live for God? How bad do you want to find your place in the kingdom? God didn't give up on David. But David could've easily given up on God like many of us do when the going gets tough. We try running away; running away to drugs, running away to alcohol, running away to bad relationships. But because David wouldn't allow his faults or his bad choices and decisions to define him he chose to repent and was able to receive restoration after his repentance. Now it's important to note here what true repentance is. Most of us seek God for forgiveness and find ourselves in the same place over and over again but proper deliverance can only happen when we honestly and truly repent of our misdoings. Namely, we can't return to the sin from which we are repenting.

Psalm 42:1-2As the deer panteth after the water brooks, so panteth my soul after thee, O God. My soul thirsteth for God, for the living God: when shall I come and appear before God? I want you God. I need you God. I hunger; I thirst for more of you in my life God. David reached for the Lord with great desire in his heart. One thing have I desired of the Lord, that will I seek after; that I may dwell in the house of the Lord, all the days of my life, to behold the beauty of the Lord, and to inquire in his temple.

How bad do you want to? How bad do you desire to be in His presence? How bad do you desire a better life than the life you've had already?

Women, What the Hell are You Thinking Now?

God reminds us in Psalm 91:1-4 that when we dwell with God in the secret place we can hide under His shadow. He will be our fortress if we just trust in Him. He will protect us from all the enemy desires to do to us. He will be our shield and out buckler. How bad do you want to be in His presence? How bad do you desire to find that secret place with the Lord?

Accessible to all who desire Him, there are no appointments necessary, no time restrictions imposed. Desiring our companionship, He's normally the one to make the first move. But we have to be up for the challenge to go higher and deeper in our relationship with Him because the enemy isn't pleased when we take a stand to follow after the higher calling. The Bible talks about going from the milk of the Word, to the meat of the Word. It's not a group decision we must each decide for ourselves when we will enter in and how far we'll go.

You need a blessing in your life, the solution to a problem that you're facing, the answer to a question in your mind, relief from a crisis situation that you are up against; you have to want to find the answer. You want to know the Lord on a greater level than ever before, a deeper relationship with the Lord than you've ever had, the gift of the Holy Ghost, your loved ones to be saved, you have to want to live the life and experience the relationship necessary to manifest these desires of your heart.

In Ezekiel 22, the Lord is speaking to his people and says: The people of the land have used oppression, and exercised robbery, and have vexed the poor and needy: yea, they have oppressed the stranger wrongfully. And I sought for a man among them that should make up the hedge, and stand in the gap before me for the land, that I should not destroy it: but I found none. Therefore have I poured out mine indignation upon them; I have consumed them with the fire of my wrath: their own way have I recompensed upon their heads, saith the Lord GOD.

When we fail to develop a close relationship with God, we rob ourselves, as well as others. We belong to Him and not to ourselves. We have a duty, an obligation, to Him to fulfill the purposes for which He created us. You have to want to be an Esther, who'll lay her life on the line, petition the king, and spare her people from annihilation. You have to want to be an Abraham, who'll stand between God and a lost people and plead for their salvation. You have to want to be a Joshua, who'll stand against the crowd and say, as for me and my house, we'll serve the Lord. You have to want to be a Moses, who'll say I chose the Lord and living for Him over the pleasures of the world. You have to want to be a marked woman, who'll cry out in travail because of the abominations being committed in our cities. Where are the priests of our homes who'll weep, and say, spare my family, my children, the people of God? You have to want to.

God is the provider of all your needs. You have to consciously decide to place your trust not in public institutions or material things; but in God. You have to want to keep your eyes on Him instead of your circumstances. In Psalms 16:8-9, David said he continually set the Lord before him, which means he looked at God and not his circumstances. David wasn't shaken. His heart was glad and he felt protected. You can experience tranquility if you want to. When your situation makes you feel unsettled check your focus. Willfully focusing on Him in Spirit and in truth, worshiping Him, and trusting Him will give you a new perspective. As you draw near to Him, you'll feel Him drawing near to you.

I'm glad that when I needed a deliverer, God came through for me in the time of need. God always has been a deliverer, especially to His people. The scripture is full of examples of His deliverance. He delivered the apostle Peter from prison. He delivered the Hebrew children from the fiery furnace. He delivered the children of Israel from Egypt with ten mighty plagues and a Red Sea crossing. He delivered Lot from the destruction of Sodom. He delivered

Daniel from the lion's den. He delivered Jonah from the belly of the whale. He delivered Paul and Silas from prison.

God is our deliverer. There's no circumstance or crisis situation that He can't bring you through. He knows just what to do when we have a problem in our life. We need to call out to him. You have to want to invest all of yourself with God.

There's a story told in the Bible about a King named Joash and Elijah the prophet. Joash was the twelfth king of Israel and the first one to at least try to move in the right direction. Early in his reign, he had apparently been in the counsel of Elijah, because when he sought Elijah's guidance later in his reign the language he used to greet the prophet showed sincere respect and reverence.

Now Joash had an opportunity to be a good king because even as Israel was still in a state of humiliation and distress, reeling from the imprudent decisions of former kings, Joash's visit with the prophet, now a man well in his eighties could have assured them victory. Joash could have turned around the Northern Tribes of Israel but he never saw the good through to completion because he simply didn't want to.

Elisha, old and sick, in a weakened condition, raises himself from his bed, drawing from his last bit of strength, the old prophetic fire burning in his eyes as he begins to speak to young Joash. As the Spirit leads the prophet, the prophet leads the king in a symbolic act of deliverance. He tells Joash to pick a bow and arrow and stand before an open window with an arrow ready to shoot. The prophet, no doubt with great difficulty, joins Joash at the window and places his hands over the hands of the king. He commands the king to shoot the arrow. Elisha declares, "That was the arrow of the Lord's deliverance, and the arrow of deliverance from Syria: for thou shalt smite the Syrians in Aphek, till thou have consumed them." Elisha told Joash that the arrows represented not only deliverance, but also victory. After all the years of oppression and humiliation, finally victory was in sight for Israel. However, the prophesy was not yet over because King Joash still had a whole lot of arrows left over. Elijah commanded him to take the arrows, the arrows of the Lord's deliverance and victory, and strike them on the ground. He struck three times and stopped. This made Elijah angry because he should've struck the ground with arrows until they were all gone. He would have struck down Syria till he consumed it, just as he had done the arrows. But the reality is Joash never really entered into the spirit of what HE and Elijah were doing. Maybe he thought he was just going along with an old man, so he stopped short of the goal and therefore only got partial results. You see the arrows were pledges of deliverance and victory from God to Joash.

But Joash stopped short of complete victory. He only asked for three victories and that's all he received. We're like Joash because we don't want to ask God for what we perceive to be impossible.

God's issue with us is not that we ask too much, or expect too much, but that we don't ask enough, and we don't expect enough. Our God is a big God and he can do big things. Joash missed a blessing because he stopped short. Are you stopping short in your life? Are there things you desire in your life that you haven't attained because you don't want them bad enough; then it's time to get God out of the box.

What would you do if I told you the next prayer you prayed would bring the answer to your need, an end to the crisis situation that you've been facing, a lasting effect upon the salvation of a son or daughter? Would you be like Joash and just hit the ground a couple of times or would you hit the ground until the answer came? Would you just pray a little prayer like you always have or would you pray until the answer came?

Maybe your family hangs in the balance, or the problems that you're having with your children would be solved, or the spiritual breakthrough you've been looking for, or the power and presence of God in your life the way you've desired, or the salvation of that loved one you've been longing to see saved hangs on the next prayer you pray. But do you want to?

Have we done everything God has for us to do, reached the place God has for us, reached our potential, reached the lost like God wants us to reach the lost, experienced the revival that God has for us? Do you want to?

You've been in a spiritual drought for too long, praying and fasting for some time seeking the face of God. These are the days we'll see the heavens rolled back and the glory of God revealed in ways we can't even imagine. God's waiting to pour out His spirit on all those who will pursue Him. He's poised to do things in and through us that will change the world as we know it.

I see the women of God growing like never before receiving a revelation of the mighty God in Christ Jesus. His Spirit poured out in great measure providing for healing and miracles taking place to the glory of God. But it all depends on you. Do you want to?

I now ask like Joshua, are you ready to possess the Promised Land. He said, "Sanctify yourselves, for tomorrow the Lord will do wonders among you." Sanctify yourself. Set yourself aside for the work of the Lord. Consecrate your life to God; "seek first the kingdom of God and His righteousness…" and God will do wonders in your life. But it all depends on if you want to.

Matthew 14:24-33, "But the ship was now in the midst of the sea, tossed with waves: for the wind was contrary. And in the fourth watch of the night Jesus went unto them, walking on the sea. And when the disciples saw him walking on the sea, they were troubled, saying, it is a spirit; and they cried out for fear. But straightway Jesus spake unto them, saying, be of good cheer; it is I; be not afraid. And Peter answered him and said, Lord, if it be thou; bid me come unto thee on the water. And he said, Come. And when Peter was come down out of the ship, he walked on the water, to go to Jesus. But when he saw the wind boisterous, he was afraid; and beginning to sink, he cried, saying, Lord, save me. And immediately Jesus stretched forth his hand, and caught him, and said unto him, O thou of little faith, wherefore didst thou doubt? And when they were come into the ship, the wind ceased. Then they that were in the ship came and worshiped him, saying, of a truth thou art the Son of God."

Peter wanted so bad to get into the presence of Jesus that he climbed out of the boat in the middle of a storm just to be near Him. The other eleven were content to wait for Jesus to come to them. My question to you is: Do you want to?

Delayed Not Denied

Habbakuk 2:3, "But these things I plan won't happen right away. Slowly, steadily, surely, the time approaches when the vision will be fulfilled. If it seems slow, wait patiently, for it will surely take place. It will not be delayed."

Have you ever wanted something so badly in life you could taste it? It may have even been something that belonged to someone else; a car, a home, a man. For you church folk, maybe it was an anointing, a voice, a prayer life. Yet, to no avail; you sought and you sought. Later on you saw that car and it was sitting in the yard because the people couldn't afford to get it fixed, or the home was being foreclosed on because there wasn't enough money to keep up the note. Maybe you saw the woman who got that man and she was living in a shelter after being beaten within inches of her life. Have you ever been frustrated with God? Have you met other people who were? Have you waited and waited for that thing to happen and it still hasn't. That husband still hasn't appeared to ask you for your hand in marriage, the baby has refused to show up. The promises of help, the job, the business breakthrough are not manifesting physically? Delayed is not denied.

I thank God for allowing me to be a witness that a blessing delayed, isn't always an indication of a blessing denied. No one believed a single teenage mother could excel. In fact, statistics said I would be on welfare the rest of my life, living in the projects, just one more black girl depleting the government of its resources. Was defeat going to be my path? It could've been. I could've chosen to blame everything and everyone around me. After all my "ex" never paid child support, the government refused to give me assistance because my parents made too much money, and my hope was fading fast. Tears flowed, my heart ached, but my prayers never ceased. I chose to speak life into my situation every chance I got. My mind kept playing the tape that hope was alive and well despite the difficulties I was facing. God wouldn't abandon me and my efforts. God had a plan for my future. He was firm in His promise mentioned in Jeremiah 29:11, "For I know the plans I have for you, declares the

Women, What the Hell are You Thinking Now?

LORD, plans to prosper you and not to harm you, plans to give you hope and a future."

I was waiting for specific fulfillment of God's plan in my life which God promised to me during my prayers. But waiting isn't easy to do. You might be waiting on your job promotion, salary increase, dream house, spouse, healing, or salvation of loved ones. I want to encourage you as you wait to meditate on God's Word revealed to us through the prophet Habakkuk. It presents us with the art of waiting for the fulfillment of God's plan in our lives. We get frustrated when there are delays. We take actions, say things and make choices that reinforce our frustration. Deciding what "we" want and believing God will do it even though we never really asked Him, "Lord, is this your plan for me in this situation," leaves us frustrated about promises that were never ours to begin with. We can believe God for each of the 3000 promises He made in the Bible, but the question is, are they made to each of us individually according to His vision for our lives? In the bible, the vision God had for Solomon was to build Him a temple. As much as David wanted to do it, and as much as he served God, he couldn't succeed at it because it just wasn't God's will for Him. When God doesn't answer right away, we become anxious and discouraged, forgetting God fulfills His promises in His own time.

His promise to Noah that there would be a great flood took over a century to fulfill. His promises to Abraham weren't even fulfilled in Abraham's lifetime. One day is like a thousand years in God's time table. Delayed is not denied. I declare to you on today, delay is over. Rethink your situation right now, and make a decision to overcome seeing your circumstances from your own point of view, and begin to see it from God's point of view. Delay is not denial. Wait prayerfully on God building your faith as you pray expectantly, consistently, and accordingly based on God's Word. Wait actively on God building up others. Read God's Word, meditate on it and spread it everywhere you go. Wait patiently on God and build your own character. It's one of the things we all find so difficult – to wait and especially to wait patiently! Busy and active, trying to keep up with our often hectic and frantic schedules is one thing, but having to wait just isn't easy. Maybe it's because we like being in control. Maybe we've waited so long we've given up, or maybe it's simply our microwave mentality. We want it now. But God reminds us to be anxious for nothing making our petitions known to Him because His plan may come slowly, but be encouraged; it will come steadily and surely. Noah waited 120 years until it began to rain. Abraham waited 99 years before Isaac came. Moses waited 40 years in the desert before the promised deliverance of Israel from

Women, What the Hell are You Thinking Now?

Egypt took place. Joseph spent several years in prison before he became ruler of Egypt. David waited until the death of Saul before he became king. Even Jesus waited for 30 years before He started His ministry. God's delay is not denial.

When we go before the Father and put up our petitions before Him, sometimes we have to wait, because God is taking us to a place where we completely surrender to His will, and trust Him to do what He must in our lives. Some of us have been waiting years for some things to come to pass, but we can't allow that negative demon to whisper in our ears we did something wrong and that's why God isn't blessing. Beloved, recognize every day you wake up as a blessing; one more chance to get it right. Don't always look for the things you want to come to pass, but start looking at the things that have already came to pass that you didn't even ask God for, those exceedingly abundant blessings you didn't even know to ask for or think about. Too often we focus on the bad, never realizing we need to thank Him in that as well, because as I've said before, all things work together for good. That job you lost, when looked at with the proper perspective, could be a setup for you to start a business or it could be an opportunity to go back to school or maybe an opportunity to spend more time with your children. Stop focusing on the storms and realize that after every rain cloud there is a rainbow; and that rainbow symbolizes God's promise to us.

When it's about to rain, we don't see anything because it becomes dark and the rain comes down hard; and depending where you are sometimes the rain hurts, and sometimes it rains so much it may even become flooded. In our walk with Christ, the trials and storms come and darkness blots out the light of day. Some trials are harder than others, some hurt real bad, others become so heavy you sink into the flood waters with no life jacket, and no rescue boat; it's just you and the Lord, but then God, the author and finisher of your faith, El Shaddai, the Almighty God, sees you and has mercy, and dries up the rain and allows the sun to shine again. He knows where every one of us is in our walk with Him, and He knows when to calm the sea. I've learned, and am still learning, that if some of our blessings are being delayed it's because God is still molding us and creating in us His perfect will, and when you receive the blessing, everybody will know that is was nobody but God. Your delay is not a denial.

People ask why I'm so transparent, and the answer is easy; "we are over-comers by the blood of the lamb and by the word of our testimony," there has to be a test in order to have a testimony. In the body of Christ, we have to realize, that it's not about us, but all about Him. Our testimonies shouldn't be hidden in an effort to make people believe we've been saved all our lives. Our testimonies are for the edification of those who may feel like giving up, feel God has forgotten about them. So through my testimony I want you to know your delay is not a denial:

Isaiah 54:4, 6-11, 13,-17, "Fear not; for thou shalt not be shamed: neither be thou confounded; for thou shalt not be put to shame: for thou shalt forget thy youth."

See, I no longer have to feel ashamed about my past, being raped and abused, because God has restored me. For the Lord hath called thee as a woman, forsaken and grieved in spirit, and a wife of youth, when thou wast refused, saith the Lord.

I was a young woman when I was first married, and I went through with my "ex", and the things he did caused me to not trust men, but God took me back.

"For a small moment have I forsaken thee; but with great mercies will I gather thee." Isaiah 54:7.

"For a while, I turned away in furious anger, but now I will have mercy and love you forever, I am your protector and Lord, and I make this promise to you. O thou afflicted, tossed with tempest, and not comforted, behold, I will lay thy stones with fair colors, and lay thy foundations with sapphires." Isaiah 54:11

God was telling me, "I know you're broken and discouraged, tossed around in the storm, but I will rebuild you with precious stones and beauty." God already knew when He was going to release my blessings. They may have been delayed, but they weren't denied.

I waited obediently on God. I was waiting for God to act, but I kept on doing the things I already knew I should be doing while I waited patiently, and the time passed quickly, because it was spent usefully and I didn't miss out on what God was doing! Don't go MIA!

I waited in expectation from God! In Luke Chapter 1, Zechariah is told by the Angel that his prayer has been heard and he will have a son. His response however is, "How can I be sure of this? I'm an old man and my wife is up in age as well?" In other words "It's too late" He believed he'd waited long enough, and the dream was all but dead inside of him. Having given up waiting for an answer to his prayer, he's shocked to find out God hasn't forgotten – the time had come!

I was expectant – even when time seemed to stand still. I laid my heart's desire before the Lord with seemingly no answer. I was reminded: though it tarry, wait for it; because it will surely come. Are you waiting today? Does it seem hopeless? Have you given up? Tired and worn out? Remember this, "But they that wait upon the Lord shall renew their strength; they shall mount up with wings as eagles; they shall run, and not be weary; and they shall walk, and not faint." Isaiah 40:31.

For our God is faithful, in His perfect timing He will do what He has promised. Delay is not Denial.

GIANTS DO FALL

Now the Philistines gathered their armies for battle and were assembled at Socoh, which belongs to Judah, and encamped between Socoh and Azekah in Ephes-dammim. Saul and the men of Israel were encamped in the Valley of Elah and drew up in battle array against the Philistines. 1Samuel 17:1-2, 1Samuel 17:4 a nd a champion went out of the camp of the Philistines named Goliath of Gath, whose height was six cubits and a span [almost ten feet]. 1Samuel 17:32 David said to Saul, Let no man's heart fail because of this Philistine; your servant will go out and fight with him.

We all face giants in our lives: unemployment, debt, disease, depression, abandonment, abuse, rejection, addiction, fear, and broken relationships. Our giants may even be yelling at us at the top of their lungs, "You're not qualified for that job! You're not good enough! You can't pay your bills! You can't save your marriage! You're losing your kids! You can't get off drugs! You'll always be on government assistance! You can't shake your past failures! You don't have a bright future! You're too dumb. You're too fat. Your life is a mistake! You should never have been born." But just like David, you can stand and face your giants using the same tactics David did. Giants do fall. In fact, the bigger they are, the harder they fall.

Perfection and people pleasing were two of my biggest giants. But God delivered me from the belief that I had to be perfect to live for Him. Wanting to be accepted and loved by all people we find ourselves with a dilemma when they don't accept us and don't love us the way we need them to. Allowing how people feel about us to cause us to miss the mark with God our lives ultimately spiral out of control "I'm sick and tired of people pleasing!" As we said before, so say I now again, "If any man preach any other gospel unto you than that ye have received, let him be accursed. For do I now persuade men, or God? Or do I seek to please men? For if I yet pleased men, I should not be the servant of Christ." Galatians 1:9-10

Women, What the Hell are You Thinking Now?

Jesus is the Son of the Father, but it didn't matter how much good He did, how many people He saved, how many people He healed, He was still hated. They hated Him because He preached and uncompromising Gospel rooted in the Word. They hated Him because there gods and their money couldn't do what Jesus did. Jesus was a radical man of God. He always went against the status- quo. It mattered not to Him what others thought He should do. Justification of who He was never bothered Him because He knew who He was and when you know who you are, you don't have to make a fuss about someone recognizing the anointing that rests upon your life. Trying to explain to "man" who you are becomes a moot point when God already knows your name and has qualified your anointing. Jesus was different. He didn't feel the need to fit in with everybody else, to be popular, and to be accepted by others. He didn't suffer from low self-esteem or self-worth, or feel like He had to "Be a part of." Jesus was different, and He was secure about himself and who He was. The only need He had was to please His Heavenly Father and not people. Not liked by many because He usually did the difficult, unlikely, unpopular things, Jesus wasn't liked by the in crowd. Jesus was rejected because He could see things people didn't want Him to see or know. Recognize that people will tolerate you as long as you're doing what they want you to do, or as long as you don't pass them up. Forsaken by His own disciples Jesus often traveled the road alone choosing to always do what the Father would have Him do. He kept it real. Our problem today is we spend far too much time trying to please everybody else. People are just people they can't determine your destination or the will of God for your life. We lose ourselves and our identities with God when we place so much emphasis on what people think or what people will say. You don't even like Prada, but you wear it because everybody else holds it in high esteem, because that's what's "In". You can't even afford the upkeep on the Mercedes you drive, or the jewelry you wear, or the fashion you buy, but you'll break your neck and go bankrupt trying to fit in, and just as soon as you obtain the next new thing, it's already old and outdated. Busy trying to make your boss happy and breaking your neck working overtime, busy trying to make your husband happy by giving in to their every little need, trying to make your children happy, your mother happy, your father happy, your boyfriend, all in the name of acceptance, but the question is, what are you doing to make God happy?

    I have wanted so badly at times to fit in. Just to be a part of something- of anything. I didn't realize that I really wouldn't fit in or couldn't fit in because I'd been called out; set apart for the work of the Kingdom. My real problem was that people's expectations of me were ever changing. They were fickle and wishy washy. When it seemed like I'd reached a person's expectations their bar of excellence was raised. People pleasing, put me in bondage, because I was always competing against them and trying to be all that they wanted me to be and because I wasn't living up to their standards, I felt bad about myself; I was insecure. But through God's grace, mercy and revelatory knowledge, I stopped allowing people to control me. God freed me from a defeated way of thinking, He'll show you too, that your voids can be filled with things that will bring growth and prosperity into your life. Ultimately, we all teach people how to treat us. We have control of whom and what we allow to be in our lives.

Facing the giants that challenge you today, requires you to know the weapons that God prepares for us. To join the battlefield called life, and be confident of God's presence, to cut off the enemies head and overcome totally all the deception of the devil in your life, you need to know how to plug in to the source of your power. Just as all our electronic appliances will be useless unless connected to the source of their power, our life is useless if we aren't connected to the source of our power and that source is God. Time and time again God's people have been empowered by the outpouring of His anointing, but far too many of us short circuit that power with our own self-doubt our own disbelief in the ability of God to deliver us.

Some would have you believe there is some kind of secret. But I heard a psalmist say there is no secret what God can do. Some would have you believe that thinking your way out of bondage is something new. But the Bible says there's nothing new under the sun. It goes on to say so a man thinketh so is he. Some would have you believe that positive affirmations are a new age way of finding success and living a joyous existence; but the Word of God has always said you have the power of life and death in your own tongue. You need to plug in to the power source that is the Word of God. Don't be like Saul who was anointed to be King, receiving all the rights and powers given such an office, only to have all that power forfeited because he deliberately sinned against God.

Giants faced in our lives are far too often created by our own selfishness and sinful choices. If you choose to smoke all your life, don't get angry with God when you get lung cancer. If you continue to engage in sexual sin, don't get angry with God when you contract a venereal disease. If you buy a house or a car that's way out of your budget, don't get angry with God when it's repossessed or foreclosed on. When you don't put God first in your marriage, don't wonder why it succumbs to infidelity, lack of communication, and poor understanding. Set yourself apart from the rest of society and take responsibility for your actions.

One of the Greek words translated sin in the New Testament means to miss the mark and not share in the prize. So when we sin, we're allowing the enemy to cause us to miss out on the will of God for our life. When sin is present in our life we can't fulfill the divine destiny that God has for us. Therefore, we surrender to our giants. James 1:14, "But every man is tempted, when he is drawn away of his own lust, and enticed." James says every man is tempted to be drawn away and enticed. You're running along with your eyes on God and all of the sudden, "BOOM", a new job paying more money but requiring you to work every Sunday and miss church comes along or a man with a good job, a nice car, but no God tempts you and your eyes look away.

Sin will take your eyes off God; come on and take a puff, take a drink, try some drugs, have a little sex, it's not church music but hey music is music, and when we finally turn to see what's behind us, we can't see our way back through the forest. We look all around and we can't see God anywhere. Where is He? Where has He gone? Oh, there He is. My eyes are back on Him. We feel pretty good because we had an encounter in the world and we still made it back to God. But when we start messing around with things that are against God's laws, it says in Genesis chapter 4 and verse 7 that, "sin lieth at the door." Personifying sin as a demon; crouching, waiting to pounce on us. We must learn to resist because sin will destroy us, ruin us, leaving us empty and broken. It looks good on the outside, but when it's finished it always leaves us ruined.

Sex before marriage looked good. It was wrapped up in dark chocolate so smooth it was irresistible; even claimed to be called to preach. The enemy knew exactly how to wrap the package up, what to say to get me hooked, but once I started unwrapping that chocolate and began to partake of its delectable goodies, the dark chocolate got bitter and it left an aftertaste that was hard to cleanse from my palate.

The enemy's deception cajoles you into believing his lies that you can mess with this for a while and still go to church, or dabble in this and still catch up to the rest of the church's ministries - it's not like we have any spiritual giants there anyway. I can have some friends out in the world - they won't influence me. Even if they do, I can still get back in the race after a while. I can do what I want to and still do what God wants me to later on in my life. You better be careful, because sometimes we can run so far, sin won't let us back in the race. The world will entangle you so you'll never be able to make it back again. There are those that say, "I can do anything I want to." They say, "I don't have to follow the standards of the church - I'm bigger than that. I don't have to follow the Word of God - I'm bigger than that. I can do my own thing and still get back in the race in time to finish." And while we're out in the world doing just what we want to, we're sacrificing the will of God and the divine destiny that He has for our life.

Do what David did. Invite God's help. Who bet on David? Who put money on the kid from Bethlehem? Not the Philistines. Not the Hebrews. Not David's siblings or David's king. But God did. And He's betting on you right now. David ran toward his giant. You should do the same! You may get knocked down a time or two, but don't quit. Keep loading the rocks. Keep swinging the slingshot. Keep your eyes focused on the target get a good aim and fire. Don't be disturbed by the giant. Don't be discouraged by the detractors. Focus on God. Listing hurts won't heal them. Itemizing problems won't solve them. Categorizing rejections won't remove them. But emphasizing God and His power will. Don't get in your own way, by trying to do things or fix things that only God can. Who's holding you up from the promises of God? Who's in your ear whispering negative things? We have to be very careful of who we allow to speak into our spirit, because even the well-meaning can be giants in our way.

Go to God and leave it with Him, don't be vulnerable to others opinions about you. Don't expect demonic spirits to be easily identified because truthfully, many times they're camouflaged and appear to be something they're not.

Ask God to do a spiritual inventory on you, you'd be surprised what comes up and what lets go once God starts cleaning you out. Seize your divine opportunity and cut off the enemies head. Cut off evil communications; elicit relationships, bad habits, drug addiction, alcoholism, dishonesty, adultery and infidelity. You are fearfully and wonderfully made, and God is the one who made you; when in doubt, ask God and He'll lead, direct, and guide you. Ultimately only what you do for Christ will last. Giants do fall.

PRAISE YOUR WAY THROUGH

"A new heart also will I give you, and a new spirit will I put within you: and I will take away the stony heart out of your flesh. And I will put my spirit within you." Ezekiel 36:26 27.

"To appoint unto them that mourn in Zion, to give unto them beauty for ashes, the oil of joy for mourning, the garment of praise for the spirit of heaviness; that they might be called trees of righteousness, the planting of the LORD, that he might be glorified." Isaiah 61:3.

The Bible speaks of the Holy Ghost as being the comforter. God will console those who mourn in Zion. There is enough of God to comfort all who mourn around the world. But His Word specifically states those in Zion, or those in God's house, are going to get God's attention.

God's people who are in: disaster, despondency, a desperate situation, mourning, trouble, hard times, difficult circumstances, will surely get His attention. And if there is anybody who I want to have their attention – it's God. I want His eyes on me, His ear tuned in to my cry. I want to be underneath the umbrella of His protection in the secret place of the most high abiding under His feathers and under His wings.

The Bible says He'll give us beauty for ashes. What does that mean? Well, in Bible times it was customary for the people of that day to lay in ashes when they were experiencing great times of mourning and difficulty. Extremely profound to imagine, you've got a problem in your life and you just sit down in a pile of ashes. Beauty is not a word that comes to the forefront when thinking of the grayish powdery residue left after something is burned.

But the scripture says, He's going to take your difficult, disgusting, depressing and horrible condition and give you beauty. He's going to pick you up out of the ash pile of life and make something beautiful out of you.

The Hebrew word for ashes is epher, and the Hebrew word for beauty is pheer. Just move the e and you have a new word and just as quickly as it takes for you to move one letter, God is going to turn your sorrow into joy. He speaks and it is already done.

Ugly and insignificant, right now rest assured all you need is the right place to grow. There is a plant known as the Century Plant. This plant grows for years with big awkward course leaves three inches thick and very long. It puts out sharp thorns and its sight is definitely not pleasing to the eye. The longer it's alive and the more it grows, it just gets more grotesque all the time. But unexpectedly it shoots up over a very short period of days, and a great shaft, tall and thick begins to grow. Its spreading head fills with thousands of flowers and it becomes a beautiful plant. Fragrant beauty was always entrenched in the repugnant ugliness, just as the fragrant beauty of your life is sometimes hidden underneath the calloused ritual, smothered by daily schedules and the monotonous grind of routine banality. Ugly experiences can cause beauty to come forth.

Isaiah said He will give you beauty for ashes. God knew you would be burnt by life's`experiences. But He also knew H% could replace that burnt out mess with something beautiful. Whatever God's hands touch becomes beautiful. All you need is a touch from the master's hand.

Let's talk about this spirit of heaviness. It includes: inner hurts, depression, dejection, hopelessness, broken hard heart, suicidal thoughts, self-pity, excessive mourning, insomnia, sorrow, or grief .The root of this spirit of heaviness can at times come from a lack of praise; bitterness not being thankful. The spirit of heaviness will attempt to steal your joy. Without it we have the tendency to move into self- pity.

Psalm 69:20 says reproach hath broken my heart; and I am full of heaviness: and I looked for some to take pity, but there was none; and for comforters, but I found none.

The devil wants you to feel sorry for yourself. He wants you to feel alone and depressed. But don't let him lead you down that pathway.

Hanging onto fear, hurt and pain can actually block the healing power of the Holy Spirit in your soul. It's important and necessary to open up and allow the Lord to heal your wounds. Our receiving inner healing from God is important to Him because His Son paid a costly price for it! Let Him set you free from the bondage that holds you down.

Isaiah 43:1-7 says, "But now thus saith the LORD that created thee, O Jacob, and he that formed thee, O Israel, Fear not: for I have redeemed thee, I have called thee by thy name; thou art mine. When thou passest through the waters, I will be with thee; and through the rivers, they shall not overflow thee: when thou walkest through the fire, thou shalt not be burned; neither shall the flame kindle upon thee. For I

Women, What the Hell are You Thinking Now?

am the LORD thy God, the Holy One of Israel, thy Savior: I gave Egypt for thy ransom, Ethiopia and Seba for thee. Since thou wast precious in my sight, thou hast been honorable, and I have loved thee: therefore will I give men for thee, and people for thy life. Fear not: for I am with thee: I will bring thy seed from the east, and gather thee from the west; I will say to the north, Give up; and to the south, Keep not back: bring my sons from far, and my daughters from the ends of the earth; Even every one that is called by my name: for I have created him for my glory, I have formed him; yea, I have made him."

These are words about a God that is concerned about you. Getting wrapped up with the process of living day to day, we lose interest in, and neglect words like these. We feel the weight of serving God because the joy is gone and we're left with the doldrums of Christian living. King Saul was affected by depression. He called for David to play and sing the anointed Psalms.

But thou, O LORD, art a shield for me; my glory, and the lifter up of mine head. Psalms 3:3.

You can give in to depression or resist it. Don't give in to the spirit of heaviness – but use the Word of God like a sword. When the devil says you're no good, remind him you were fearfully and wonderfully made.

When the devil says you're not saved just tell him I know I'm saved because I believe in Jesus the Christ. He is my savior and I have confessed Him to be my Lord. When the devil says to worry, just remind him that God said be anxious for nothing. When the devil says be sick, just tell him by His stripes, I am healed. When he says be afraid, remind him God said He didn't give you the spirit of fear and He has promised to give you perfect peace. When he says be defeated, you say we are more than conquerors through Him that loved us.

Victim mentality says life has treated you unfairly; the whole world's against you, troubles in life are a punishment. This train of thought rarely allows you to take responsibility for your feelings, failures, behaviors, or actions. Honestly, bad things happen to good people and life is unfair, but don't give in to the temptation to wallow in defeat.

Praise is a garment of the spirit. Put on the garment of praise, for the spirit of heaviness. Literally clothe yourself in praise, put it on every morning--decide what to wear.

In Hebrew, the word used for garment was more than something draped around the shoulders, but it literally teaches us to wrap or cover ourselves in praise. The garment of praise is to leave no openings or holes where hostile spirits can penetrate. Praise prepares us for miracles. Put on the garments of Praise.

The Hebrew word – tehillah means to sing praise. It's used in Psalm 22:3 where it says God inhabits the praise of his people. God manifests himself in the midst of passionate praise.

Isaiah 60:18..."but thou shalt call thy walls Salvation, and thy gates Praise."

God is surrounded in a city, by a wall called salvation. The way to get into that city is through the gate of praise. If you want to enter into the presence of God, needs and petitions are not the answer. Instead praise your way through. To receive His peace, His joy, His blessing, enter into His gates with thanksgiving and into His courts with praise.

Ezekiel 36:26-27 reminds us, "A new heart also will I give you, and a new spirit will I put within you: and I will take away the stony heart out of your flesh...And I will put my spirit within you."

Spiritual transplants do occur, but only God can perform the operation. God's spiritual surgery can take your broken heart and broken spirit and make it new. I'm not telling you something I heard; but something I know. Just like any surgery, there is a healing process and when God removes certain seeds that were planted in you; He has to pull them from the root. Once a root is removed you'll find a hole only God can fill. Trying everything you can, will only lead you to fill the void with God. Why do we go to the hospital and listen to the doctor, taking the medicine he prescribes for pain, but we always second guess God's medicine? My God is a healer and restorer. Allow Him to do the same thing with you. Praise your way through.

Love Your Neighbor as Yourself

"That ye put off concerning the former conversation the old man, which is corrupt according to the deceitful lusts; and be renewed in the spirit of your mind; and that ye put on the new man, which after God is created in righteousness and true holiness." Ephesians 4:22-24.

Love your neighbor as yourself. We've all heard this saying before. But what happens when you don't love yourself? Learning to love you starts with making a conscious decision, an intentional choice to become happy and lead a fulfilled life. When you don't love yourself and suffer from low self-esteem, it's almost impossible to ever reach the God-given potential that's on the inside. Loving yourself means you accept that you're responsible for the outcomes that you experience in your life and would like yourself to shine from living a fulfilling life.

The amount of bondage that results from self-rejection, self-hatred, and unwillingness to forgive oneself is overwhelming to say the least. Can you honestly look in the mirror and tell yourself, "I love you" and mean it with your heart? I'm not talking about in a prideful way, but an humble means of accepting who God has formed in you. We need to love and accept the person that Christ has made in us, and forgive ourselves as Christ has forgiven us!

When you look inside, you hate yourself, you could kick yourself over and over for your past failures and choices you believe there is no hope for redemption or transformation. You've come to Jesus and repented, but you haven't really accepted the truth about what Jesus has done for you because it seems so unbelievable that a gift that precious would be given so freely. In fact you not sure you've even forgiven yourself! You still feel ashamed and guilty over your past and you keep holding it against yourself. The way you see yourself is not an accurate picture of what Christ has done for you. It is basically denying the work that Jesus accomplished for you on the cross! If your sins are forgiven, then you need to see yourself as separated from your sins...but know, the enemy will try his very best to remind you of your past and continue to beat you up over sins that were supposed to be nailed to the cross. You are wrapped up in guilt and condemnation; women of God, you need to forgive yourself and move on. You can go through deliverance, but if you don't forgive yourself for the mistakes you've made, you won't experience the breakthrough that you need in order to be totally set free.

When a person receives a gift and receives it with joy and gladness, the giver is lifted up and glorified. But when the gift is received and tossed aside or ignored, the giver is overlooked, belittled and feels unappreciated. The minute you gave your life to Christ, the person you once were disappeared forever; a perfect example of that is Saul, more commonly known as the Apostle Paul. He was the Pharisee's Pharisee. H knew the law better than most people of that time. Because of it he persecuted, murdered, and defiled thousands of believers. Hated and feared by Jews no one would've ever believed that God could use someone like him in His service. But one day on the road to Damascus, Paul had an experience that changed His life forever. He is a testimony to the transforming power of a living God.

God's grace was revealed in the life of Paul over and over again according to his desire to live for God. You too are not beyond redemption. God wants to use you, but you have to know who you are, and whose you are beyond a shadow of a doubt. You have to love the God that's in you. Forget those things that are behind you and press toward the high calling in Christ Jesus.

Be honest with yourself. Realize that down deep inside, you're not happy with the person of your past. If you're in denial, then forget trying to treat the root of your problem. You need to see the problem before you can apply the solution. To help you do so make a list of all of the things you hate about your past and one-by-one, give them to God and release yourself from each one.

Your debt has been paid in full by the One who loved you more than you love yourself. You can't continue to beat yourself up, after Jesus has paid your debt, unless you aren't accepting the gift He's freely given to you. Accept what Jesus has done for you by faith. The price for your redemption has been paid in full. It's up to you to receive it and realize that the blood of Jesus actually removes the sin from your record. Now see yourself as being forgiven and justified. Holding on to self-hate, self-doubt, and self-pity blocks the Holy Spirit's power from entering and healing that area of your mind and life! Allow the Holy Spirit to heal you. Open up your heart; allow the light of Christ to shine into the darkness of your soul. See the "new creature" of Christ within you. If you've repented of your past, and sought God's forgiveness, then you are forgiven or justified. You don't have to forget what happened, but don't remind yourself of it either. See your past through your spiritual eye rather than you natural eye and see how this changes everything!

Failing to see yourself as God's Word sees you, is denying the very work that Jesus did for us when He suffered, and died on our behalf. Don't let this continue in your life another day...accept the free gift of God and begin to see yourself as a new creation in Christ, who's past failures have been purchased with the precious Blood of Jesus!

If you hate the person that you are, but God's Word tells you you're a new creation that's been washed clean with the Blood of Christ, whose "past" has been purchased with the work that Christ did on the cross... do you hate that person? Do you despise the new creation God's made you? Or are you still a sinner in need of salvation? Are you in Christ or not?

Romans 8:1, "There is therefore now no condemnation to them which are in Christ Jesus, who walk not after the flesh, but after the Spirit."

Love yourself in a balanced way. Do your best but don't expect perfection or you'll always be disappointed and frustrated. Believe in your value, necessity, and talents. Change the way you think about people. They won't all like what you like, want what you want, or think like you think, but it's okay they're not supposed to. You are free from comparison. Do you want to bring glory and honor to Jesus? Then accept His gift with great joy, and begin to see yourself as that new creation...begin to see your past failures as being "paid in full" by the great sacrifice that Christ made for you. Begin to see you the same way that your Heavenly Father sees you!

Love Yourself!

BACK TO YOUR FIRST LOVE

*S*ay unto wisdom, Thou art my sister; and call understanding thy kinswoman: That they may keep thee from the strange woman, from the stranger which flattereth with her words. For at the window of my house I looked through my casement, And beheld among the simple ones, I discerned among the youths, a young man void of understanding, Passing through the street near her corner; and he went the way to her house, In the twilight, in the evening, in the black and dark night: And, behold, there met him a woman with the attire of an harlot, and subtle of heart. She is loud and stubborn; her feet abide not in her house: Now is she without, now in the streets, and lieth in wait at every corner. So she caught him, *and kissed him, and with an impudent face said unto him, I have peace offerings with me; this day have I paid my vows. Therefore came I forth to meet thee, diligently to seek thy face, and I have found thee. I have decked my bed with coverings of tapestry, with carved works, with fine linen of Egypt. I have perfumed my bed with myrrh, aloes, and cinnamon. Come; let us take our fill of love until the morning: let us solace ourselves with loves. For the good man is not at home, he is gone a long journey: He hath taken a bag of money with him, and will come home at the day appointed. With her much fair speech she caused him to yield, with the flattering of her lips she forced him. He goeth after her straightway, as an ox goeth to the slaughter, or as a fool to the correction of the stocks; Till a dart strike through his liver; as a bird hasteth to the snare, and knoweth not that it is for his life. Hearken unto me now therefore, O ye children, and attend to the words of my mouth. Let not thine heart decline to her ways; go not astray in her paths. For she hath cast down many wounded: yea, many strong men have been slain by her. Her house is the way to hell, going down to the chambers of death.*

Look at the woman in this story. Is this the kind of woman you want to be; a home wrecker, an adulteress? Well, that's what you are when you sleep with someone else's husband. There is no justification under the sun that can make this situation okay. God's Word suggests that He clearly frowns upon this type of behavior. Quite frankly, those of you that have been hanging on to married brothers should step back and re-evaluate the relationship that you are in. Why do you continue to devalue yourself? You should not want to be second to another woman. The commitment of marriage is a sacred one and you are assisting in the degradation of a covenant with God. How can you possibly expect to be blessed? Furthermore, if he (the man) cheated once, he'll do it again, because he knows that if you were desperate enough to be with him in the first place, (knowing that he was married), you'll be desperate enough, like his wife, to allow him to step out on you.

Life is full of temptation. It generally comes from two sources, our own desires and Satan. Satan is the father of all lies. He distorts the truth to tempt us. How often have you heard these lies, "I'll leave my wife for you baby;" or "My marriage is in the pits, we don't even sleep in the same bed together," or "We're only together for the children." When we allow Satan to cause us to give in to this temptation, we sin against God. This sordid lifestyle will keep you from inheriting the kingdom of God.

Know ye not that the unrighteous shall not inherit the kingdom of God? Be not deceived: neither fornicators, nor idolaters, nor adulterers, nor effeminate, nor abusers of themselves with mankind. I Corinthians 6:9-11. The good news is that God is still a forgiving God, and if you ask him through prayer and supplication, He can help you master one of the most elusive fruits of the spirit; self-control. God allows us to be tempted to teach us obedience, trust, and loyalty to Him. Remembering God's Word will help us to resist Satan. Using the word of

God is the most effective way in which to overcome temptation. When we submit ourselves to God through obedience, He will equip us with the strength to fight the devil. Self-Control is a personal decision. It allows us to say 'no' to things that are not of God. Believe me; sleeping with someone else's husband is not of God! Pray to God for self-control and discipline. You can be forgiven and freed from the tricks of the devil. "And such were some of you: but ye are washed, but ye are sanctified, but ye are justified in the name of the Lord Jesus, and by the Spirit of our God." I Corinthians 6:11. You must stop giving men all the power and return to your first love.

Jeremiah 6:16-17, this is what the LORD says: "Stand at the crossroads and look; ask for the ancient paths, ask where the good way is, and walk in it, and you will find rest for your souls. But you said, 'We will not walk in it.' I appointed watchmen over you and said, 'Listen to the sound of the trumpet!' But you said, 'We will not listen."

Women, What the Hell are You Thinking Now?

Getting away from the basics will always get you into trouble. A passage in Revelation talks to the Pastor of the church in Ephesus. Ephesus was the capital of the province of Asia. It was called "The Light of Asia." It was the ending point for a great system of Roman roads that constituted the trade route westward. It was famous for the great "Temple of Diana," one of the Seven Wonders of the World. Ephesus was also the hotbed of every false, religious cult and superstition known to man at the time. It was in this city that was filled with paganism that God planted a church to shine the Gospel light throughout Asia. The Church that was in Ephesus had a great Christian background Paul started it, John the beloved was the pastor for a time and Timothy was also there for a period of time. This church was blessed with great leadership.

In the Lord's message to Ephesus in Revelation 2, He said some very good things about this church first: It was commended as being active and energetic because the people had many activities in the church. They were in "business" for the Lord, they labored at cost. Things weren't always easy for the church in this pagan city because they were confronted with all kinds of trials and tests. Yet they were patient and accepted their difficult situation. They were sensitive to evil, which meant they couldn't bear them that were evil. Their spiritual discernment, their endurance, their determination, their stable, and sound doctrine as a church; yes, they had a lot to be commended for. But then the Lord says, I do have something against you because you have "left" your first love. Something had happened to this church that left it cold, mechanical, and routine. They weren't experiencing the Love of God as they once had, and they had become comfortable with routine, ritual and tradition. Hard work, sacrifice, doctrine and hatred of evil wasn't enough. They had left their first love. An entire church had entered into a backslidden condition devoid of intimacy and devotion to God even as they continued to work hard for him and stay doctrinally pure and obey all of the standards of the church. The same is also evident in the lives of some Christians, who while working hard for God; they have somehow distanced themselves from Him. Choosing to leave their first love and leaving their spiritual passion behind, because of the lifestyles they lead Christian's can find their way back to God by making better choices.

Nothing is more important than your relationship with God. Yet sin, in its very essence, is an assault on that relationship. That's why sin must be uprooted, broken, hated, and rejected. Sin's goal is to steal that one thing in life you can't live without – relationship with God; and it will separate you from your savior. You can lose your friends, your possessions, and your health, but if you lose your relationship with God, all of the friends, all of the possessions, and all of the physical strength in the world will never buy you one moment of true joy or satisfaction in your life. Only Jesus can satisfy your soul. Knowing Him must be your highest goal. Having a relationship with the almighty God must be on the top of the list of your priorities. If not, then when temptation comes and blows against your life, it will expose a house without a foundation and a tree without roots. The house will fall with a crash, and the tree will crumble into the dirt. Don't leave your first love. Don't leave your relationship with God.

We were created to know and serve the Lord; to walk with Him, to enjoy Him, and to work for Him. But as a people, we have chosen instead to go our own way, looking to find satisfaction and fulfillment in: money, achievements, food, sex, education, family, work, and religion to name a few. Still, there's a hole in our spirits so large we spend our entire lives looking to fill it; a wound that can't be healed, a heart cry that can't be comforted. Only God can fill that hole, mend that wound, and dry the tears of the heart cry!

Our relationship with God must be the most valuable thing in our lives. Go back to your first love.

THE DEVIL MADE ME DO IT

Then Moses stood in the gate of the camp, and said, who is on the LORD'S side? Let him come unto me. And all the sons of Levi gathered themselves together unto him. Exodus 32:26. If my people, which are called by my name, shall humble themselves, and pray, and seek my face, and turn from their wicked ways; then will I hear from heaven, and will forgive their sin, and will heal their land." 2 Chronicles 7:14.

I've had the opportunity to minister to hundreds of women who've lost their jobs, or who've experienced the pain of bad relationships; and I've concluded we give the devil too much credit. The devil's not the one who gets us in all of our mess, some of the mess we're in we got into all by ourselves. The devil didn't have anything to do with it. You started showing up late for your job and not completing the tasks you were given, that's why they laid you off; it didn't have anything to do with the devil. You don't like your living situation, but the devil didn't have anything to do with it. The Lord didn't tell you to move into a home you couldn't afford, you didn't consult with Him. Your relationship is complex and difficult to live with, but you didn't allow the Lord to direct your path. Nobody told you to date that man, but you just had to be with him because you thought he was so fine. You thought you could change him, but he ended up changing you. The Bible says that Solomon loved many strange women. He had seven hundred wives and princesses, and three hundred concubines. The Lord said, don't get mixed up with those strange women, and don't get mixed up with those strange men. They began to worship idol gods and they did evil in the sight of the Lord, just like David, his father. He began to worship those idol gods and built a temple and burned incense unto them.

    The Bible says acknowledge Him in all your ways and He shall direct your path. But we want to acknowledge the Lord in some of our ways, and not all of our ways. We want to acknowledge Him in our healing, but not in our daily living when we buy a car or when it's time to look for a mate. When I lost my job, I didn't stay home and watch the young and the restless. I was the young and the restless. Getting a new job became my job. I got up in the morning, got dressed, made phone calls, faxed resumes, and went on interviews. You have to be persistent, you have to be diligent, and you have to be hopeful. When responses didn't come in right away, I took it upon myself to identify business opportunities and eventually started my own agency. Where there's a will, there's a way. We want to be successful, but we don't want to work at it. The only place you can find success before work is in the dictionary and encyclopedia or thesaurus; not in life.

A lot of Christians haven't tapped into the power that God has placed on the inside; and that's why the enemy continues to trip them up with the same problems. Until we find out who we are in Christ, the devil will continue to chase us instead of us chasing the devil. That was an epiphany for me, and even though he still tries to hinder me, I know the power I have to tear him and his kingdom down. Without knowledge of the Word and its teachings on how to resist the devil you simply entertain him, and reinforce his belief that he can do what he's come to do, and that's to steal kill and destroy.

2 Corinthians 10:3-5, "For though we walk in the flesh, we do not war after the flesh: For the weapons of our warfare are not carnal, but mighty through God to the pulling

down of strongholds; Casting down imaginations, and every high thing that exalteth itself against the knowledge of God, and bringing into captivity every thought to the obedience of Christ."

Having the power God has given me, I acknowledge I don't have to keep getting beat by the enemy over and over again. I let him know I've canceled every assignment he's placed on me, my family, and anyone else that comes in contact with me. I stand bold in the enemies face and let him know I declare victory, and I let him know I'm not trying to climb the mountain because I have the power to speak to the mountain hindering me and tell it to get out of my way! He's studied me for a long time, but I don't allow him to intimidate me. I take the armor of God with me:

If you want to get out of your mess, God said you have to be my people and called by my name. You have to pray and seek the Lord's face. You have to turn from your wicked ways; stop smoking your weed, stop snorting your cocaine, stop your trickin', stop being promiscuous, stop your lying, stop your backbiting and stop your gossiping and negativity. Stop doing anything that will take you out of the will of God. Turn from your wicked ways, turn your back to unrighteousness, and turn your back from un-holiness. Turn away from what you know is wrong and walk through the straight gate. Narrow is the way of the Lord and wide is the path to destruction. The Bible says that we have to lay aside every weight and sin that so easily besets us. Get rid of that dead weight. The sins belong to the devil, you belong to GOD.

Having a repentant heart, making up your mind that you're sorry for your sin leads you to the path of righteousness. Jesus said, "I didn't call the righteous, but sinners to repentance." Repentance is defined as deep sorrow or regret for wrongdoing. Real repentance, true repentance, can only lead to an ultimate hatred for sin. The bible says that if you delight yourself in the Lord, He will give you the desires of your heart. He also said He is a rewarder of them that diligently seek Him. If you want to get out of your mess, you have to humble yourselves get rid of your pride and learn how to ask somebody for help.

As I was raising my children, I often found myself in need trying to make ends meet. For a long time I resisted the temptation to ask for help, but I eventually realized if I wanted to get out of my mess, I had to learn to be humbled and not proud. I learned to seek the help of others and to seek help from the Lord.

Lord I've messed up, I've made some bad decisions, but I want you to deliver me, I want you to direct my path. Lord I'm sorry I didn't consult you first.

If you want to get out of your mess, trust in the Lord and you will be successful.

Lord, I want to get out of my mess. Many are the afflictions of the righteous, but the Lord shall deliver them out of them all. I have got to get out of my mess. I shall outlast my struggles. I have to be like Jacob, and say, 'Lord, I'm not going to let you go until you bless me.' I'm going to hold on to the Lord all night long.

Stop blaming the devil.

Transform Your Thinking to Transform Your Life

"I beseech you therefore brethren, by the mercies of God, that you present your bodies a living sacrifice, holy, acceptable to God, which is your reasonable service. 2 And be not conformed to this world, but be transformed by the renewing of your mind, that you may prove what is the good and acceptable and perfect will of God." Romans 12:1-2.

Satan relentlessly seeks to build strongholds in our minds. But he's a liar and he only twists the truth. He deceives. But the good news is, we have weapons with which to defeat him. The spiritual war we're fighting requires us to open our spiritual arsenal of weapons and put on the whole armor of God; because this war can't be fought in a normal way. We can't hit, shoot, strangle or the enemy up. We can't put Satan in jail; but we can defeat him when we use the right tools.

We need only to look at the example Jesus gave to identify the most powerful weapon we have. You see when the Spirit led Jesus into the wilderness, Satan immediately tried to tempt Him and make Him question who He was, but instantly after every attempt of the enemy, every lie of Satan, Jesus used the Word of God to rebuke him and cast him away. The Word is God's manual for life and when applied properly to each and every situation we face it brings deliverance. God's Word is His will and it's only when you seek His plan over your situation that you can achieve the success and fulfillment you desire. His Word is foundational. It's the road map that guides you to your divine destination, without it any path you take will lead you to a dead end.

Before you can truly transform your life, you have to become established in the truth of God's Word and understand the role it plays. When our minds are consumed with the Word of God, it opens us to transformation which in turn, moves us closer to the will of God; His true intentions for us. Easier said than done, we find ourselves regularly responding to situations in our lives more like the world, than like Jesus, because deceived minds lead to deceived lives. It's these very responses that put barriers and limitations on God's ability to act on our behalf. It's a well-known fact the deepest recesses of the mind are where life's fiercest battles are either won or lost and abundant living can only be achieved when you intentionally walk with an undefeated attitude. So, the question I ask you is, "What are you thinking? What's on your mind that's reflecting in your actions?"

By allowing the Word to guide you, you will make significant progress. God's Word is the starting point of everything, and it promises to bless and empower you for real. Don't continue to let your lack of knowledge concerning the Word; hinder you from life-changing breakthroughs.

Women of God, we've been set apart, and our thinking shouldn't be like that of the world. Worldly wisdom isn't worth anything if it doesn't line up with Godly wisdom. You see, reasoning causes us to deceive ourselves. The worldly person, not the believer, is the one who should want to understand everything mentally. Some won't believe or don't believe because they can't see God or figure Him out. They want control of their own lives. Not believing in God is often just an excuse for not being willing to change lifestyle habits. But the Word says in Romans 10:10-11, "With the heart (not the mind) a person believes and is justified and made right with God." We should have a different logic, a different mind-set than the world. We should have a compassionate mind, a consecrated mind, a careful mind that causes us to think more of others than ourselves, die to our flesh daily, and be on guard as to what we subject our minds to. This transformation of our mind and our thoughts should give us a different mission and purpose from that of the world. Our lives should be lived in service and sacrifice to God and not ourselves. Sacrificing our time, our talent, and our treasure is what will keep our thoughts focused on the important things of God that bring about kingdom living. If your life is a mess, then your thinking is probably a mess, because you've allowed Satan to use your mind as a dumping ground.

When our thinking has been transformed we're not the same person we used to be. We have different companions, ones who'll encourage us, not entangle us. Our hearts desire is to now be in the world, but not of the world. Our speech now conveys God's grace. It preserves and doesn't destroy. Transformed thoughts, replace irrational assumptions that we have to be loved and accepted by those who are most important to us. A transformed mind understands that we don't have to be perfectly competent and successful in our achievements before we can be happy with ourselves. When transformation takes place you know longer believe it's easier to avoid certain difficulties and responsibilities rather than face them because you now know the truth of the Word that says, "Blessed are you when men revile you and persecute you and say all kinds of evil against you falsely on my account. Rejoice and be glad, because great is your reward in heaven, for in the same way they persecuted the prophets who were before you." Matthew 5:11and12. "Such confidence as this is ours through Christ before God. Not that we are competent in ourselves to claim anything for ourselves, but our competence comes from God. He made us competent as ministers of a new covenant - not of the letter but of the Spirit, for the letter kills but the Spirit gives life." 2 Corinthians 3:4-6. Truthfully, too many of us assume that our well-being is based on being loved and accepted by people. We predicate our achievements on our ability and competence alone, rather than acknowledging God equips us, energizes us, and enables us to be competent for everything He asks us to be, do and think.

    Thoughts that tell you, I'm bad and deserve punishment and blame for my sins, or that you've been shaped by the past and it's too late to change, must be counteracted with the knowledge that Jesus interceded for people just like you and I who need to grow up in all spiritual, emotional, and mental dimensions instead of condemning them. You don't have to be a prisoner to the past. Let the past be passed away.

A serious transition of the mind and transformation of the heart that leads to leaving your baggage behind along with the pain and suffering of the past requires you to be fully persuaded about the Biblical promises of God. If you're determined to break the generational curses and dysfunction, and you truly want to grow in God, your healing and freedom depend on how quickly you accept what He has to offer and believe it in your heart. Proverbs 4:23 says it best, "Guard the affections of your heart for they affect every area of your life." If you want to see a change in your life – change your beliefs first. Jesus said, "You will know the truth and it will set you free." John 8:32.

Expose the lies of the enemy. If you're feeling afraid, ask yourself what you're thinking. If you're sad, ask yourself what's in your mind that caused it and change your thoughts about the situation by reading, listening, studying, meditating, and memorizing the Word of God. Saturate your mind with Scripture, think His thoughts about you, and you'll be amazed how your feelings become secondary, as the truth of God permeates your mind, your body, and your soul. Your belief patterns are in your mind. Every time you think about a belief, it becomes more deeply embedded in your psyche, until over time a mindset is formed. If you want to change that, and align it back to God's truth permanently, you have to constantly feed on the truth of God's Word! Occupying your mind with the truth leaves the enemy no room to fill it with his lies.

Transformation and the renewing of the mind involves real soul searching and truth telling, both of which can be difficult to endure because it demands we look at ourselves in a way that's introspective, objective and relevant. If we're honest, most of us don't want to deal with our faults or distorted belief structures and issues. Yet, this is the only way we can make our way to the kind of thinking that results in a clear vision of what God wants for our lives.

When the pressures of life bring areas of dysfunction to the forefront, this is when we examine ourselves and reflect on our foundation. Changing our behavior alone won't work because the behavior isn't the root of the problem; our thoughts are.

Conformity to this world instead of transformation in the light of the world to come, is a daily struggle for the believer because before we came to Christ we lived according to the flesh because it felt good and we wanted to. But because we were born again, when we accepted Christ, we no longer live according to our old carnal selves, but according to the Spirit of God which is now in us. You are now a co-heir with Christ, a sinner saved by grace with the hope and promise of eternal life in heaven. But here's the dilemma: we must choose to live either according to the Spirit or the flesh and we have to choose daily. We find ourselves inquiring daily what would Jesus do? We must be cautious, active, alert, and watchful. We can't afford to be passive, lazy, or wishful in our thinking.

What does Satan say? You're worthless and useless, and God is angry at you because you just can't do things right. He says, there's no hope and no future, because you're powerless, so you should just give up. If you believe this, you're destined for a defeated presence just as the woman who believes that success is decided by wealth and possessions and thus she lives her life accordingly. Relationships, marriage, family, and other foundational aspects of life are cheapened by the world and we tend to follow suit. What you think dictates how you live. What you feed your mind will ultimately be seen in how you live. If you neglect the spiritual food of the mind, then you'll end up living a Christian life of weakness and ultimately famine. A life of fear, predicated upon what the devil says to you, or shows you, and replete with all the doubt, double mindedness, and unbelief you can handle. But when we consistently renew our minds, we no longer think like an unbeliever. We no longer feed our minds on the things we once did, but on things which build us up, strengthen our faith and encourage others. Paul says, when we do this, we will be able to discern the will of God for our lives.

But so many of us are unsure, ignorant and blind to the will of God; not because we don't want to know His will, but because we don't have the spiritual mind to know it. We've starved our minds of spiritual food. Consequently, for some the pages of Essence, Cosmopolitan and the Wall Street Journal have made bigger change in their lives than the Bible ever has. Fashion, the media, popular psychology, folk religion and superstition has changed lives more than the truth of the gospel. Why is that?

Beloveds, there are no shortcuts to spiritual growth or maturity. There's no easy route to renewing a mind and transforming a life, in fact it's a painful lifelong path.

How do we then begin the journey? How do we transform our thinking to transform our lives? The answer is multifaceted, but concentration is a good place to start. Concentration on that which is pure, that which is holy, that which is edifying, and that which pleases God, keeps us in a consistent mindset that's positive, empowering, and uplifting. Eliminating from our minds that which is impure, not edifying, not conducive to helping us pursue a life of victory, and not what God would be pleased with us dwelling or focusing on, allows us to concentrate on right living. It's a lot like parents who cover their children's eyes in the movie theater because they don't want them seeing nudity or other obscenities. The same is true of us as believers; if we're not careful what goes into our minds ends up coming out in our actions. If what goes in is bad and dirty, then our actions will probably be also. However, if the opposite is true and what we feed our minds is good, what's right, then we're much more likely to do what's right. Focusing our thoughts in the right place, on the good things spoken of in Philippians 4, allows us to maintain the right mindset. Truth turns our attention away from the darkness and secrets, and reminds us not to spend our time inquiring things that do not concern us, but instead on those things which are delightful to God, build character, and are glorifying to God as we spend our time thinking about it.

    Our thoughts should be on honorable things that are dignified. What we are to think about should have attributes of divinity, purity. The idea here is that we should focus our attention on that which reflects God's character, in accordance with His nature, His righteousness, His purity. Thinking rightly on that which is upright, virtuous, observant of divine laws and focusing our attention on that which agrees with Scripture and God's standard of purity and virtue leads us on a path of righteousness. Thinking purely on that which excites reverence, that which is sacred, chaste, modest, pure from carnality, clean, unstained, focusing our attention on that which would never cause someone to blush, things I wouldn't mind my grandmother knowing I was thinking about looking at or listening to should be our daily focus.

When I'm thinking lovely thoughts that express and exhibit a loving character and loving actions, then I don't have time to listen to gossip or hate talk or racial jokes...or anything that demeans another person.

When I'm thinking thoughts of good repute, which give a favorable report acknowledging those things which edify, rather than tear down; which are positive rather than negative, which lifts up rather than demean, that foster a good report or good reputation concerning someone then I don't have time to berate, belittle, or talk about anyone else.

When my thoughts are excellent, virtuous, modest, and pure; when they are on those things that are untainted, that are modest rather than extreme, and of the highest standard I don't have time to allow my body to be misused and abused by someone who has no intentions of keeping me a virtuous woman.

When my thoughts are praiseworthy and commendable, thoughts of higher things than just what's "acceptable," more than just the minimum standard then a welfare poverty mentality has no room to reside in my mind.

Deliberately filling our minds with that which is honorable, lovely, excellent, and positive is advantageous, unfortunately from television, radio, music, media, teachers/professors, neighbors, false teachers, and more we're still exposed to outside stuff that perpetrates the truth by putting up a beautiful facade that lures us into its inner sanctum. Knowing how to respond to these outside forces, we have no control over gives us more power and authority to succeed in life. Learn to apply the principle found in 2 Corinthians 9:5 -- "...we are taking every thought captive to the obedience of Christ."

If there were a stranger entering your gated community, would you rather authorities allow him to stay without checking any credentials or identification, while they look on to see what he's going to do and they do nothing until he's done doing damage, or would you rather they interrupt him, capture him, force him to identify himself, get rid of him if he's unfriendly and only allow those persons to enter your space that are friendly, well meaning, and harmless? Well, of course no one would stand for a system that lets us be harmed and then just "analyzes the damage" afterward. Instead, we want a system that interrupts and challenges, stops or destroys those persons trying to cause us harm. That's also the kind of defense system the Bible tells us to employ when it comes to our thoughts. Simply put, we need to be skeptical of anything presented as "friendly" or "truth" until we've carefully examined it and compared it to what we know is truth; the Word of God. Never are we to allow anything to take root in our thoughts, unless it is pleasing to God. Likewise, 1 John 4:1 tells us "...do not believe every spirit, but test the spirits to see whether they are from God, because many false prophets have gone out into the world."

Satan is the author of lies and we must be vigilant in recognizing those lies when they present themselves. The best way to call the devil out on his lies is to test it with the Word of God. If the words spoken or the principles presented don't line up with the Bible then it's not truth regardless of whose lips it may come from. It is never necessary for one to manipulate, explain, reconstruct, or otherwise smooth over the truth. When you deny the deity of Jesus, the Divine inspiration of the Bible, and purport that there are many ways to God, which are all in direct opposition to Bible doctrine, then I know it's only a trick of the enemy to get me away from the truth. In fact, Scripture itself warns us that Satan himself will pose as an "angel of light,"(remember he wasn't thrown out of hell he was thrown out of heaven) a preacher of truth, when he's actually the father of lies.

Truth will always stand on its own despite what the majority rules. The only determining factor in this case is God. Just because a lie has been told over and over again, doesn't make it true; it's still a lie. It's imperative that we study God's Word so we'll know how to discern between that which is truly true, as opposed to that which merely presents itself as true: Casting away from our thoughts anything that is not pure, which does not glorify God. "Taking every thought captive to the obedience of Christ destroying speculations and every lofty thing raised up against the knowledge of God" isn't easy. There's a real battle going on...a battle for your mind...a battle for your thoughts...a battle being waged by Satan and his unholy spirits, the forces of evil, against the influence of the Holy Spirit of God. Living a holy life, a life pleasing to God, begins with thinking holy thoughts, guarding our minds from that which is unholy, not pleasing to God, and that which would inevitably lead to unholy actions.

Going outside the boundary of that which is true in some situations can be a good thing an in the case of an artist or a writer, a performer or an inventor. Things like Disneyland, Microsoft, and the I-Phone were brought about by the ability to "dream big," they were outside the usual limits of thinking. Nonetheless, when we talk about theology and moral correctness regarding matters such as the nature of

Women, What the Hell are You Thinking Now?

God or the purpose of life and what's absolutely right or wrong, we need to stick to God's definitive and final word on those subjects, not man's imagination. Therefore, we can't give in to the imagination of men like Joseph Smith because his theology is not the truth of God. There are not "many paths" to God. It's not enough to just do good works. Good workers can be fatally wrong. Not everyone is going to heaven. Including those sanctimonious folk who go to church, sit on the front pew every Sunday, clap their hands, say hallelujah, and then cuss at folk when they can't get out of the parking lot first. In fact, the Bible clearly tells us everyone that cries, "Lord, Lord" won't enter the kingdom of heaven.

Our works are not enough. We need to cast away, cast out, cast down, destroy, anything that is contrary or contradictory to the Word, not glorifying to God, is anti-Scripture. These thoughts and ideas are without validity. They are not the truth. Why cast these things away and not allow them to take root in our thoughts? Because "garbage in" leads to "garbage out." It's not surprising that many violent crimes committed by lawbreakers in our society are a direct reflection of the actions of violent television programming or video games. Furthermore, it's not a surprise that young men who listen to gansta-rap tend to hold women in lower esteem than other young men. Why is this not surprising? Because if you fill your mind with garbage, negative images, wrong stereotypes, degrading and demeaning material, those wrong ideas will in the end affect your actions. The question we should be asking ourselves about these materials before giving our attention and focus to them is: "Does this stuff meet the standard of being pure, lovely, of good report?" If it does, then that's great. If not, then we need to cast it away.

1 Corinthians 10:31,"Whether, then, you eat or drink or whatever you do, do all to the glory of God." "If I advocate this as truth, will God get the glory? Will people be drawn to Him?" "If Jesus were to walk in while I was reading this, or watching this, or listening to this, or saying this, or doing this would He be pleased?" If so great! If not, don't watch it, don't read it, don't listen to it, don't say it, don't do it. Instead, cast it away because our example is Jesus.

John 8:29 -- "He Who sent Me is with Me; He has not left Me alone, for I always do the things that are pleasing to Him." If I were to learn that Jesus was reading this, or watching this, or listening to this, or saying this, or doing this would I be disappointed in Him? If not, great. If so, however, why do you think it would be okay for you to do it cast it away! The bottom line is we're to cast away that which disagrees with Scripture. That's what Scripture itself teaches us:

Women, What the Hell are You Thinking Now?

Romans 13:12-14, "...lay aside the deeds of darkness...and make no provision for the flesh in regard to its lusts." Ephesians 4:22-24, "...lay aside the old self...and be renewed in the spirit of your mind, and put on the new self, which in the likeness of God has been created in righteousness and holiness of the truth." James 1:21, "Therefore, putting aside all filthiness and all that remains of wickedness, in humility receive the word implanted..."

If your life isn't going in the direct you'd like it to right now, look at what you're thinking. Identify the areas where you haven't been successful and take some time to reflect about your ability to progress in that area. Comply with, and apply to your life the things of God you've learned from Scripture. Make a conscious effort to surrender your life to Christ, each day. He has made it plain that those who truly love Him will keep His commandments. The only way to do that is to die to self daily and bring your flesh under submission.

James 1:22, "But prove yourselves doers of the word, and not merely hearers who delude themselves." We need to concentrate, capture and compare, we need to cast away, comply and apply. But, finally, we need to continue this process for each thought from here on. We must listen to 2 Thessalonians 3:13, and not become weary in our well doing because God has said we will reap a harvest.

Right thinking is a life-long pursuit...with the key word being 'pursuit'...it's a continuous process. It's not a sprint, it's a marathon. It's lived daily, it's lived moment to moment and if we're serious about transforming our lives, then we must, and will commit ourselves to guarding our thoughts and filling our minds with only those things that will sustain us. Capturing and casting out false teaching. Rejecting truth simply because others might think it's so, or just because it's a popular idea begins with pursuing positive thoughts. It means applying what we've just learned. God wants you to think like He does by planting His thoughts into your mind. Do so by getting His Word, keeping it in front of your eyes, in your ears, and coming out of your mouth. Programming your mind with the Word will set you on the path to a transformed life; the ultimate battle being for the Kingdom of God that lies within you. By keeping your mind guarded against the enemy you will protect your heart and reap the harvest you really want. All of the tools mentioned in this book are available as part of our ministry in helping each person continue to grow by pursuing truth. Frankly many of you as parents are more protective of what your children view, than you are of your own minds and hearts, and yet you are then making decisions, eternal life changing decisions, for yourself and your families.

The reality is if you fill your mind with the things of this world you will conform to this world and fit into it without so much as a second thought.

Expect favor, peace and the manifested presence of God. Expect grace, gifts, strength, health, and prosperity. Expectancy fights despair. A transformed mind is the forerunner of a transformed life. Learn to think like God in every area of your life and His will be released in every area of your life. God wants to give back to us everything the devil has stolen. He wants to restore us to His original plan for our lives, a position of authority. When we have transformed out thinking it will be seen in our lives. We will begin to do what is right and make right choices. We will no longer act from a place of greed and self-centeredness.

As you begin your journey of transformation let me encourage you to do these things: enter into and participate in a Bible-reading plan. Be part of a small group Bible study. Check out the daily devotionals on the Worth More than Rubies website each day. The reason it's there is to help focus attention on that which is edifying and which will help us stay focused on God's will and God's goodness to us. I have placed a reading list on the website that includes books I've personally found helpful in my own walk. These books were useful in helping me to fill my mind with that which could help me grow spiritually in knowledge and maturity. Tune in each Tuesday to the "Titus 2 Tuesday" radio broadcast, 8:00pm-9:00pm CST on Blog Talk Radio on-line at http://www.blogtalkradio.com/worthmorethanrubies. Or, you can listen to my podcast on http://www.thewinonline.com/shows/worth-more-rubies.

Acquire the companion resources to "Women What the Hell are You Thinking Now? And utilize them to regularly to transform your thinking and transform your life. Secondly, daily prayer and Bible reading is essential if you want to renew your mind, to know the will of God, and be transformed. That requires discipline of time and it requires determination, because all sorts of things will pop up to monopolize your time. Make it a priority each day to spend time in God's Word and in God's presence in prayer. Thirdly, find a covenant partner for spiritual growth. Make sure it's someone you can trust, someone you can relate to and invite them to hold you accountable to daily bible reading and prayer. Jesus never sent His disciples out on their own – it was always two by two. Remember Doubting Thomas when he went off on his own, he had to wait another week to see the risen Christ, and he was rebuked for his unbelief. Finally, feed your mind with the things that are

Women, What the Hell are You Thinking Now?

wholesome. Become disciplined about what you watch, what you read, what you listen to and what you say.

You are what you think you are. Women what in hell are you thinking?

Practical Applications

Journaling is something I've done all my life. It has been helpful in maintaining my positive outlook on life because I can always go back to it and refer to a particular stage in my life and see how God has prospered and delivered me. Use the following practical tips to help you create the positive thinking necessary to transform your life.

1. Identify those things you wish to have manifested in your life, then go to the Word and locate scriptures pertaining to those desires. Confess these scriptures over your life daily.

2. Pay close attention to the negative thoughts in your mind. Locate scriptures that counteract these thoughts. Write them down on a 3 x 5 card. Begin memorizing the scriptures. Every time you have the negative thought recite the scripture until it becomes internalized.

3. Choose areas in your life that you want to change. Look up scriptures related to these areas and begin confessing them over your life. For example if you want improvement in your finances, look up scriptures related to finances and recite them daily. Don't forget to apply those, such as Malachi 3, as necessary. Use a journal to write down your testimonies related to breakthroughs that have occurred as a result of your obedience.

Now that you have pulled the lies out–just as you pull a weed out of the ground, an empty hole remains where the weed was, and you will need to fill the space you cast the lie out of with Scripture. Begin to think on the scriptures or confessions found on the following pages. Make a conscious effort to fill your mind with good, pure, wholesome, and lovely thoughts such as these and watch your life begin to change.

Confessions for Who You Are in Christ

Colossians 2:10

I am complete in Him Who is the Head of all principality and power.

Ephesians 2:5

I am alive with Christ.

Romans 8:2

I am free from the law of sin and death.

Isaiah 54:14

I am far from oppression, and fear does not come near me.

1 John 5:18

I am born of God, and the evil one does not touch me.

Ephesians 1:4; 1 Peter 1:16

I am holy and without blame before Him in love.

1 Corinthians 2:16; Philippians 2:5

I have the mind of Christ.

Philippians 4:7

I have the peace of God that passes all understanding.

1 John 4:4

I have the Greater One living in me; greater is He Who is in me than he who is in the world.

Romans 5:17

I have received the gift of righteousness and reign as a king in life by Jesus Christ.

Ephesians 1:17, 18

I have received the spirit of wisdom and revelation in the knowledge of Jesus, the eyes of my understanding being enlightened.

Mark 16:1718; Luke 10:1719

I have received the power of the Holy Spirit to lay hands on the sick and see them recover, to cast out demons, to speak with new tongues. I have power over all the power of the enemy, and nothing shall by any means harm me.

Colossians 3:910

Women, What the Hell are You Thinking Now?

I have put off the old man and have put on the new man, which is renewed in the knowledge after the image of Him Who created me.

Luke 6:38

I have given, and it is given to me; good measure, pressed down, shaken together, and running over, men give into my bosom.

CONFESSIONS FOR FINANCES

Galatians 3:13

Christ has redeemed me from the curse of the law (Poverty, sickness, and death).

2 Corinthians. 8:9

For poverty he has given me wealth, for sickness He has given me health.

Psalm 119:25

It is true unto me according to the Word of God.

Psalm 37:4

I delight myself in the Lord and He gives me the desires of my heart.

Luke 6:38

I have given and it is given unto me pressed, shaken together and running over.
2 Corinthians. 9:8

I have sufficiency in all things and abound to all good works, for all grace abounds toward me.
Philippians 4:19

There is no lack, for my God supplies all my needs according to His riches.
Psalm 23:1

The Lord is my shepherd, I do not want.

Chronicles 1:12

Wisdom and knowledge are granted you. And I will give you riches, possessions, honor, and glory, such as none of the kings had before you, and none after you shall have their equal.

Chronicles 31:21

And every work that he began in the service of the house of God, in keeping with the law and the commandments to seek his God [inquiring of and yearning for Him], he did with all his heart, and he prospered.

Deuteronomy 29:9

Therefore keep the words of this covenant and do them that you may deal wisely and prosper in all that you do.

Deuteronomy 8:17-18

Women, What the Hell are You Thinking Now?

And beware lest you say in your [mind and] heart, My power and the might of my hand have gotten me this wealth.

But you shall [earnestly] remember the Lord your God, for it is He Who gives you power to get wealth that He may establish His covenant which He swore to your fathers, as it is this day.

Confessions for Encouragement

1 Samuel 12:16

"...stand and see this great thing which the Lord will do before your eyes..."

Luke 18:27

"The things which are impossible with men are possible with God."

Numbers 23:19

"God is not a man that He should lie. Has He said, and will He not do it?"

James 1:4

"But let patience have its perfect work, that you may be perfect and complete, lacking nothing."

Romans 8:31

"If God be for us, who can be against us?"

2 Timothy 2:1

"...be strong in the grace that is in Christ Jesus."

2 Timothy 1:13

"Hold fast the pattern of sound words...in faith and love..."

Colossians 1 3:2

"Set your mind on things above, not on things on the earth."

Colossians 3:23

"Whatever you do, do it heartily, as to the Lord and not to men..."

Mark 9:23

"If you can believe, all things are possible to him who believes."

Joshua 1:9

"Be strong and of good courage; do not be afraid, nor be dismayed, for the Lord your God is with you wherever you go."

1 Chronicles 22:18

"And has He not given you rest on every side?"

2 Chronicles 20:17

"You will not the salvation of the Lord, who is with you..." need to fight this battle. Position yourselves, stand still and see

John 16:33

"In the world you will have tribulation; but be of good cheer, I have overcome the world."

Romans 8:18

"...consider that the sufferings of this present time are not worthy to be compared with the glory which shall be revealed in us."

Romans 8:37

"Yet in all these things, we are more than conquerors through Him who loved us."

Romans 8:39

"Nothing can separate us from the love of God which is in Christ Jesus our Lord."

Romans 8:28

"And we know that all things work together for good to those who love God, to those who are the called according to His purpose."

2 Timothy 4:5

"...be watchful in all things, endure afflictions, do the work of an evangelist, fulfill your ministry."

2 Timothy 4:7

"Fight the good fight, finish the race, and keep the faith."(paraphrased)

Micah 7:8

"Do not rejoice over me, my enemy; when I fall, I will arise; when I sit in darkness, the Lord will be a light to me."

Philippians 4:13

"I can do all things through Christ who strengthens me."

1 John 4:4

"You have overcome them, because He who is in you is greater than he that is in the world."

Philippians 1:6

"Be confident of this very thing, that He who has begun a good work in you will complete it until the day of Jesus Christ..."

Philippians 4:4

"Rejoice in the Lord always. Again I say, rejoice!"

Confessions for Needs

Matthew 6:8

"...your Father knows the things you have need of before you ask Him."

Psalms 34:10

"...those who seek the Lord shall not lack any good thing."

Psalms 24:1

"The earth is the Lord's, and all its fullness..."

Psalms 50:10

"...every beast of the forest is Mine, and the cattle on a thousand hills."

Genesis 18:14

"Is anything too hard for the Lord?"

Matthew 7:7

"Ask, and it will be given to you; seek, and you will find; knock, and it will be opened to you."

Romans 8:32

"He who did not spare His own Son, but delivered Him up for us all, how shall he not with Him also freely give us all things?"

Psalms 37:5

"Commit your way to the Lord, trust also in Him, and He shall bring it to pass."

Luke 6:38

"Give, and it will be given to you: good measure, pressed down, shaken together, and running over will be put into your bosom."

Ephesians 3:20

"...God is able to do exceedingly abundantly above all that we ask or think, according to the power that works in us..."

Philippians 4:19

"And my God shall supply all your need according to His riches in glory by Christ Jesus."

2 Peter 1:3

Women, What the Hell are You Thinking Now?

"His divine power has given to us all things that pertain to life and godliness, through the knowledge of Him..."

Jeremiah 33:3

"Call to Me, and I will answer you, and show you great and mighty things, which you do not know."

Jeremiah 32:27

"Behold, I am the Lord, the God of all flesh. Is there anything too hard for Me?"

Matthew 11:28

"Come to Me, all you who labor and are heavy laden, and I will give you rest."

Hebrews 13:5

"For He Himself has said, I will never leave you nor forsake you."

Philippians 4:6

"Be anxious for nothing, but in everything by prayer and supplication, with thanksgiving, let you requests be made known to God; ..."

2 Corinthians 9:10

"...may He who supplies seed to the sower, and bread for food, supply and multiply the seed you have sown and increase the fruits of your righteousness ..."

Psalm. 20:4

"...may He grant you according to your heart's desire, and fulfill all of your purpose."

Ephesians 1:3

"Blessed be the God and Father of our Lord Jesus Christ, who has blessed us with every spiritual blessing in the heavenly places in Christ..."

Confessions for Self Esteem

Psalm 139:13-14 ESV

For you formed my inward parts; you knitted me together in my mother's womb. I praise you, for I am fearfully and wonderfully made. Wonderful are your works; my soul knows it very well.

Isaiah 43:4 ESV

Because you are precious in my eyes, and honored, and I love you, I give men in return for you, peoples in exchange for your life.

1 Samuel 16:7 ESV

But the Lord said to Samuel, "Do not look on his appearance or on the height of his stature, because I have rejected him. For the Lord sees not as man sees: man looks on the outward appearance, but the Lord looks on the heart."

Song of Solomon 4:7 ESV

You are altogether beautiful, my love; there is no flaw in you.

1 John 3:1 ESV

See what kind of love the Father has given to us, that we should be called children of God; and so we are. The reason why the world does not know us is that it did not know him.

Genesis 1:27 ESV

So God created man in his own image, in the image of God he created him; male and female he created them.

1 Peter 2:9 ESV

But you are a chosen race, a royal priesthood, a holy nation, a people for his own possession, that you may proclaim the excellencies of him who called you out of darkness into his marvelous light.

Romans 12:3 ESV

For by the grace given to me I say to everyone among you not to think of himself more highly than he ought to think, but to think with sober judgment, each according to the measure of faith that God has assigned.

Women, What the Hell are You Thinking Now?

Matthew 11:28-30 ESV

Come to me, all who labor and are heavy laden, and I will give you rest. Take my yoke upon you, and learn from me, for I am gentle and lowly in heart, and you will find rest for your souls. For my yoke is easy, and my burden is light."

1 Peter 3:3-4 ESV

Do not let your adorning be external—the braiding of hair and the putting on of gold jewelry, or the clothing you wear— but let your adorning be the hidden person of the heart with the imperishable beauty of a gentle and quiet spirit, which in God's sight is very precious.

Mark 12:31 ESV

The second is this: 'You shall love your neighbor as yourself.' There is no other commandment greater than these."

John 3:16-17 ESV

"For God so loved the world, that he gave his only Son, that whoever believes in him should not perish but have eternal life. For God did not send his Son into the world to condemn the world, but in order that the world might be saved through him.

John 3:16 ESV

"For God so loved the world, that he gave his only Son, that whoever believes in him should not perish but have eternal life.

James 4:6 ESV

But he gives more grace. Therefore it says, "God opposes the proud, but gives grace to the humble."

Philippians 2:3 ESV

Do nothing from rivalry or conceit, but in humility count others more significant than yourselves.

Psalm 139:1-24 ESV

To the choirmaster. A Psalm of David. O Lord, you have searched me and known me! You know when I sit down and when I rise up; you discern my thoughts from afar. You search out my path and my lying down and are acquainted with all my ways. Even before a word is on my tongue, behold, O Lord, you know it altogether. You hem me in, behind and before, and lay your hand upon me...

2 Peter 1:5 ESV

Women, What the Hell are You Thinking Now?

For this very reason, make every effort to supplement your faith with virtue, and virtue with knowledge,

Ephesians 2:10 ESV

For we are his workmanship, created in Christ Jesus for good works, which God prepared beforehand, that we should walk in them.

Galatians 6:4 ESV

But let each one test his own work, and then his reason to boast will be in himself alone and not in his neighbor.

1 Corinthians 1:1-31

Paul, called by the will of God to be an apostle of Christ Jesus, and our brother Sosthenes, To the church of God that is in Corinth, to those sanctified in Christ Jesus, called to be saints together with all those who in every place call upon the name of our Lord Jesus Christ, both their Lord and ours: Grace to you and peace from God our Father and the Lord Jesus Christ. I give thanks to my God always for you because of the grace of God that was given you in Christ Jesus, that in every way you were enriched in him in all speech and all knowledge...

Romans 3:23 ESV

For all have sinned and fall short of the glory of God,

Romans 8:31-39 ESV

What then shall we say to these things? If God is for us, who can be against us? He who did not spare his own Son but gave him up for us all, how will he not also with him graciously give us all things? Who shall bring any charge against God's elect? It is God who justifies. Who is to condemn? Christ Jesus is the one who died—more than that, who was raised—who is at the right hand of God, who indeed is interceding for us. Who shall separate us from the love of Christ? Shall tribulation, or distress, or persecution, or famine, or nakedness, or danger, or sword?...

Matthew 16:24-25 ESV

Then Jesus told his disciples, "If anyone would come after me, let him deny himself and take up his cross and follow me. For whoever would save his life will lose it, but whoever loses his life for my sake will find it.

Acts 10:34-35 ESV

So Peter opened his mouth and said: "Truly I understand that God shows no partiality, but in every nation anyone who fears him and does what is right is acceptable to him.

Confessions for Faith

Romans 12:21

I am the body of Christ and Satan has no power over me. I overcome evil with good.

1 John 4:4

Greater is He that is in me, than he that is in the world.

Psalms 23:4

I will fear no evil, for you are with me Lord, Your Word and Your Spirit comfort me.

Isaiah 54:14

I am far from oppression and fear does not come near me.

Psalm 1:3

Whatsoever I do shall prosper for I am like a tree planted by rivers of water.
Galatians 1:4

You have delivered me from the evils of this world, for it is Your will.
Psalms 91:10

No evil shall befall me; neither shall any plague come near my dwelling.
Psalms 91:11

For You have given Your angels charge over me, and they keep me in all my ways.
Proverbs 12:28

In my pathway is life and there is no death.
James 1:25

I am a doer of the Word of God and I am blessed in my deeds.
Ephesians 6:16

I take the shield of faith, and stop everything the enemy brings against me.
Galatians 3:13

Christ has redeemed me from the curse of the law; I forbid sickness to come upon me.
Revelation 12:11

I overcome by the blood of Jesus and the word of my testimony.

Women, What the Hell are You Thinking Now?

James 4:7

The devil flees from me because I resist him in Jesus's Name.

Psalms 119:89

The Word of God is forever settled in heaven.

Isaiah 54:13

Great is the peace of my children for they are taught of the Lord.

ABOUT THE AUTHOR

Someone once asked Cheryl Lacey Donovan what her passion was in life, I said, "God has given me a heart for women who are struggling with life's twists and turns. My message to them is even when we can't diagnose the problem; God's word can bring us healing and wholeness. I want to bring this message to all women. I want them to understand that until they fall in love with Jesus, the chains of sin and bondage will never be broken."

CHERYL LACEY DONOVAN

Cheryl Lacey Donovan has developed a unique voice that manifests itself through her literary endeavors. Her newest contribution, *Women What in Hell are You Thinking Now: Transform Your Thinking to Transform Your Life,* compels women to look at themselves and their lives and take inventory. If they don't like what they see then it's time to clean the clutter.

Welcome to the world of Cheryl Lacey Donovan.

www.cheryllaceydonovan.org

Peace In The Storm Publishing, LLC is the winner of the 2009 & 2010 African American Literary Award for Independent Publisher of the Year.

www.PeaceInTheStormPublishing.com

CHERYL LACEY DONOVAN

Get these companion resources for
Women What the Hell are You Thinking Now?

Transform You Thinking to Transform Your Life CD
Transform Your Thinking Worship and Affirmation CD
Transform Your Thinking to Transform Your Life Devotional Journal and Workbook
Confessions for Life Devotional

Visit
http://www.worthmorethanrubiesministries.worpdress.org

Have Cheryl speak at your next event or host a Worth More than Rubies event featuring Cheryl Donovan

cheryl@worthmorethanrubiesministries.org

832-525-0651

ENJOY THESE PEACE IN THE STORM PUBLISHING TITLES:

Walk a Mile by Ebonee Monique
Caught In The Middle by Jacqueline D. Moore
A Whisper to a Scream by Elissa Gabrielle
Ask Nicely and I Might by Lorraine Elzia
Dorothy by LaToya S. Watkins
Giving up the Ghost by Stacy-Deanne
Serving Justice by Jacqueline D. Moore
The Ministry of Motherhood by Cheryl Donovan
Mistress Memoirs by Lorraine Elzia
A Whisper to a Scream by Elissa Gabrielle
Hiding in the Shadows by Claudia Brown Mosley
Suicide Diaries by Ebonee Monique
The Baker's Dozen by S.D. Denny
Holy Seduction by Jessica A. Robinson
Good to the Last Drop by Elissa Gabrielle

And Many More…

www.ingramcontent.com/pod-product-compliance
Lightning Source LLC
Chambersburg PA
CBHW031245290426
44109CB00012B/439